ELIE WIESEL

Ted L. Estess

FREDERICK UNGAR PUBLISHING CO.
NEW YORK

For S. P. E.

C . 1

Estess, Ted L   1942-
    Elie Wiesel.

    Bibliography: p.
    Includes index.
    1.   Wiesel, Elie, 1928-   —Criticism and inter-
pretation.
PQ2683.I32Z67   813'.54   80-5337
ISBN 0-8044-2184-6

549393

Portions of this book, in a considerably different form, have
appeared in *The Journal of Religion* and *Soundings.* They
are included here with the permission of these publications.

Biblical quotations are from the *Holy Scriptures According to the Masoretic Text* (1917; Philadelphia: Jewish Publication Society of America, 1955).

Acknowledgments

I am indebted to the Research Office of the University of Houston Central Campus for a grant that assisted me in completing this project. I appreciate also the contribution that several persons have made. Elie Wiesel has befriended me, first with the gift of his work, and more recently with conversation. Stephen Langfur has spent many hours listening and responding to my thoughts about the issues with which this book deals. Allen Mandelbaum and John Bernard read the manuscript and made helpful suggestions. Mary-Violet Burns and Maria Albright helped with the typing. I am grateful to these persons, friends all. And to Sybil P. Estess, to whom this volume is dedicated, I am thankful in ways that take a lifetime to unravel.

Contents

Chronology

1928   Elie Wiesel is born in Sighet, Rumania, on
            September 30. (Transylvania, the region in
            which Sighet is located, is annexed by Hungary
            in 1940, and it reverts to Rumania in 1945.)

1934–1944   In Sighet, Wiesel goes to *heder* (primary
            school) and later to a yeshiva, where he
            becomes a diligent student of the Torah and the
            Talmud.

1944–1945   Wiesel is a prisoner in German concentration
            camps (Birkenau, Auschwitz, Buna, Buchen-
            wald) from April, 1944, to April, 1945.

1945   He is taken to France with other children sur-
            vivors of the camps.

1946   Wiesel goes to Taverny, near Paris. He later
            takes a room in Porte Saint-Cloud in Paris. He
            earns money by working as a choir director and
            as a Bible teacher.

1948–1951   Wiesel studies philosophy, literature, and
            psychology at the Sorbonne.

1948   Working as a journalist, Wiesel visits Israel to
            report on the Israeli struggle. In the following
            years, he continues to live in Paris and to work
            as a newspaper correspondent. His work in-
            volves extensive traveling.

1956   Wiesel settles in New York, where he remains
            today. *Un di Velt Hot Geshvign (And the World*

Has Remained Silent), an account of Wiesel's experience in the Holocaust, is published.

While working as a correspondent to the United Nations for *Yediot Aharonot,* an Israeli newspaper, Wiesel is struck by a taxi in Times Square. Later, unable to get his French travel documents extended, he applies for American citizenship.

1957   Joins the *Jewish Daily Forward,* A New York Yiddish newspaper, as a writer of feature articles.

1958   *La Nuit* appears in France. In 1960 the book appears as *Night* in the United States.

1960   *Dawn (L'Aube)* is published.

1961   *The Accident (Le Jour)* is published.

1962   *The Town Beyond the Wall (La Ville de la Chance)* is published. Wiesel wins the Prix Rivarol and the National Jewish Book Council Award.

1963   Wiesel becomes a United States citizen.

1964   *The Gates of the Forest (Les Portes de la Forêt)* is published. Wiesel stops working as a journalist and devotes himself full time to his writing and lecturing.

1965   Wiesel visits the Soviet Union during the Jewish High Holy Days. His impressions of Soviet Jewry appear first as a series of articles for *Yediot Aharonot.* These are collected and published in 1966 as *The Jews of Silence.*

1968   Wiesel's first drama, *Zalmen, or the Madness of God,* is published in France. (It is first staged, as *The Madness of God,* in Washington, D.C., in 1974.) *A Beggar in Jerusalem* is published and is awarded the *Prix Medicis,* one of France's most distinguished literary prizes.

1969   Wiesel marries Marion Erster Rose, a Viennese, who is also a survivor of the concentration camps. She becomes the translator of most

of Wiesel's books. Their son, Shlomo Elisha, is born in 1972.

1970   *One Generation After* is published on the twenty-fifth anniversary of Wiesel's liberation from Buchenwald.

1971   *Souls on Fire (Célébration Hassidique: Portraits et Légendes)* is published. It consists of lectures originally given at the Sorbonne and at the Young Men's Hebrew Association in New York.

1972   Appointed Distinguished Professor of Jewish Studies at the City College of New York.

1973   *The Oath (Le Serment de Kolvillàg)* and *Ani Maamin* are published.

1976   *Messengers of God: Biblical Portraits and Legends (Célébration Biblique)* is published.

1978   Wiesel is appointed Andrew Mellon Professor of Humanities and University Professor at Boston University. *Four Hasidic Masters and Their Struggle Against Melancholy* and *A Jew Today* are published.

1979   *The Trial of God,* Wiesel's second drama, is published. Wiesel is appointed Chairman of the President's Commission on the Holocaust.

1

Never Shall I Forget

In March of 1944 Adolf Eichmann, one of the planners of Hitler's Final Solution to the "Jewish problem," moved into a suite in the Majestic Hotel in Budapest. Until that time, the seven hundred-fifty thousand Jews of Hungary had existed in an enclave apart from the Nazi cataclysm that had engulfed so much of Europe. Eichmann took a few weeks to complete his plan. In April the Hungarian police, instructed by the SS, began the work. Several months later, four hundred thousand Hungarian Jews were gone, victims of the Nazis' death factories.

Eichmann's plan included the Jews of Sighet, a town in Transylvania (then in Hungary, now part of Rumania) not far from the Rumanian border. On a day in April these Jews were rounded up. Later, they were deported, and after a long journey by cattle train, they arrived at Auschwitz. Elie Wiesel was one of the Jews from Sighet, and he was one of the few who lived to tell the story. About his first hours in Auschwitz, he writes:

Never shall I forget that night, the first night in camp, which has turned my life into one long night, seven times cursed and seven times sealed. Never shall I forget the faces of the children, whose bodies I saw turned into wreaths of smoke beneath a silent blue sky.

> Never shall I forget those flames which consumed my faith forever.
>
> Never shall I forget that nocturnal silence which deprived me, for all eternity, of the desire to live. Never shall I forget those moments which murdered my God and my soul and turned my dreams to dust. Never shall I forget these things, even if I am condemned to live as long as God Himself. Never.

Beginning on this night, Elie Wiesel spent eleven months in German concentration camps. The physical agony was horrible, the mental and spiritual anguish overwhelming. His mother and younger sister, Tzipora, were killed by the Germans, and his father died with Elie looking helplessly on. Two older sisters, Beatrice and Hilda, survived, but millions of other persons did not. To the task of remembering the many who died and the few who survived Elie Wiesel gives his life and work. On nearly every one of his pages, we detect the resolve: "Never shall I forget that night."

I

Elie Wiesel was born on September 30, 1928. The date in the Hebrew calendar was Tishre 23, Simchat Torah, an important holy day in the Jewish year.[1] On this day, the community joyously celebrates the beginning of the annual cycle of weekly Torah reading. Simchat Torah and the festival day that precedes it, Shmini Atzeret, mark an ending and a beginning. The festival faces toward the past and toward the future.

· So it is with Elie Wiesel. His life spans a breaking point in history. Looking back before the Holocaust, he sees a life in Sighet that was joyous and calm, and ordered by the quiet rhythms of the seasons and the

sacred patterns of Jewish life. This early experience—from 1928 to April, 1944—fills Wiesel with
nostalgia, so that everywhere in his work we find a
yearning to recover the life that was tragically and ir-
redeemably destroyed. "It sometimes seems," he
says, "that ever since I left it, I have been spending
all my time telling about this town which gave me
everything and then took it all away."

Wiesel's father was a practical man of reason. A
hard-working merchant, Shlomo Wiesel was not
especially religious, although he did observe the
Jewish traditions. "As for my father," Wiesel
remembers, "he scarcely spoke to me about the laws
governing the relations between man and his creator.
In our conversations, the *Kaddish* was never mentioned. Not even in camp. Especially not in camp."
But Shlomo Wiesel was nonetheless involved with the
affairs of the Jewish community in Sighet, and during
the early years of the war, he spent three difficult
months in jail for assisting Jews to escape the Nazis.

Sarah Wiesel bequeathed to her son a different
sensibility. The daughter of a Hasid, she cared more
for the things of the spirit and of the past than did her
husband. Hers was the way of faith, of mysticism, and
of fervent devotion. "It was she," Wiesel remembers,
"who brought me to *heder* to make me a good Jew,
loving only the wisdom and truth to be drawn from
the Torah. And it was she who sent me as often as
possible to the Rebbe of Wizsnitz to ask his blessing
or simply to expose me to his radiance."

Sarah Feig Wiesel gave more than an attitude of
simple faith to her children. She was also, Wiesel has
commented, "a highly cultivated person." One of the
few Jewish girls in the region to complete high school,
she admired Goethe and Schiller and other German
writers. She was hesitantly open to the modern
world. Wiesel recalls: "Her dream was to make me

into a doctor of philosophy; I should be both a Ph.D. and a rabbi."

Other influences on Wiesel's life tended to strengthen the side of faith. Most prominently, there was his maternal grandfather, Dodye Feig, who lived in Bocsko, a village close to Sighet. The grandfather would come to celebrate the High Holydays with Wiesel's family. From him, the young boy absorbed a love for stories and for storytelling. Wiesel remembers:

> A fabulous storyteller, he knew how to captivate an audience. He would say: "Listen attentively, and above all, remember that true tales are meant to be transmitted—to keep them to oneself is to betray them." He knew how intently I listened; he must have known that I would remember, but he had no way of knowing how closely I would follow his advice.

Many years later, Wiesel celebrates his grandfather with a book, *Souls on Fire* (1972).[2] There, many of the legends that Wiesel first heard from Dodye Feig come to life again, so that the words and sentiments of this simple farmer, this gentle Hasid, echo in his grandson's writing.

Elie Wiesel's early years were filled with study and prayer. Not given to dallying with childhood friends, he devoted himself fervently to studying Torah, often studying for ten to twelve hours a day. His teachers, about whom he poignantly writes in *Legends of Our Time* (1966), instilled in him a respect for language and a love of the past, and they encouraged the disciplined intensity that later dominated his life and work. Like that of many Jewish youngsters in Sighet, most of his education was religious in character. He was enrolled in a secular high school in Sighet, and he went periodically to the nearby towns of Debreczen and Nagyvarad to

take examinations. But he spent most of his time with the sacred texts, hoping to become worthy of the gifts he had received from his religious tradition.

Though tucked away in the Carpathian mountains, Sighet provided many treasures that were important in the shaping of Elie Wiesel as a storyteller. The culture induced in him a respectful, almost reverential, attitude toward language. It was a rich linguistic milieu in which to grow up. Yiddish was Wiesel's native tongue, and in it he heard the stories of Dodye Feig and received the blessing of the Hasidic masters. The family also spoke Hungarian; in this language Wiesel's father conducted much of his business. Since Sighet was part of Rumania until 1940, Rumanian was also heard and spoken. In addition, Wiesel learned ancient and modern Hebrew, the former to enable him to study the sacred writings, the latter at the insistence of his father and Yerachmiel, a childhood friend and ardent Zionist. Later, after the war, since he already knew the language, Wiesel was able to work as a correspondent for an Israeli newspaper.

The most important of Sighet's treasures for Elie Wiesel was its Jewishness, especially its Hasidism. Hasidism arose as a Jewish reform movement in the eighteenth century and later spread over Eastern Europe and into the Ukraine. For the Hasid, divine presence is everywhere, in everything; hence the devotee is to be constantly alert to recognize the holiness present in all things. Although it borrowed ideas and practices from a variety of sources, Hasidism developed a distinctive form of Jewishness that emphasized a total dedication of life to the worship of God.

Hasidism is especially indebted to the teaching of Isaac Luria Askenazi, a sixteenth-century Kabbalist.[3] A central component of his vision was the myth of ex-

ile and redemption, which teaches that "divine sparks"—variously interpreted as the "divine presence" or as God Himself—are dispersed through all the world. By his actions, man can "lift up" or "redeem" these divine sparks and restore them to God Himself, thereby restoring harmony to creation. Hence, the redemption of the world depends to a large extent on what man does.

Young Elie Wiesel sought to be true to the Hasidic vision of the universe. The ideal of sanctity captured his imagination, just as the traditions of his people held his memory. He yearned to be instrumental in the redemption of the world. For a time he attached himself, for spiritual guidance, to a Kabbalist master who encouraged the young Wiesel's tendency to withdraw from the world. Whereas a gentler form of religious feeling would have emphasized that the blessings of the spirit always come through material things—hence material things and physical existence are to be prized—the sterner religion taught by his Kabbalist master led Wiesel to harsh practices of world denial and self-restraint.

In *Legends of Our Times,* Elie Wiesel recalls his adolescent religious fervor:

With Itzu Goldblat, a goldsmith and the son of a goldsmith, I shared an ambition as naive as it was boundless: to hasten the coming of the Messiah. We were obsessed by it. Caught up in the Kabbala and its practices, we used our free time to mortify our bodies by fasting and our thoughts by silence. . . . Only internal fulfillment concerned us. Our incantations went on for hours. In the street they took us for sleepwalkers. Before every service, we made our way to the *mikvah,* to the ritual baths, to purify ourselves, otherwise our pleas would never reach their destination.

This religious intensity was being defined precisely at the time—the early 1940s—when the

smoke of Nazi crematories was drifting across Europe. Wiesel's religious devotion made the experiences he was soon to undergo in the shadow of those crematories all the more shattering to him.

His religious strictness combined with a love of words and a fidelity to texts to lead the young Elie Wiesel to write. When he was twelve or thirteen years old, he wrote a commentary on a part of the Bible. Even if there had been no war he might still have been a writer, most likely a writer of Biblical and Talmudic commentaries.

But of course there was a war, which brought the life of Sighet to an end. Today in Sighet there are fewer than fifty Jewish families. All but one synagogue are gone. Jews Street is now called "The Street of the Deported," although the population already forgets who was deported.

But Elie Wiesel remembers. That is his mission, his task, his justification for existing. With him and with his writing, "all roads lead home." Sighet, he says,

... remains the only fixed point in this seething world. At times I tell myself that I have never really left the place where I was born, where I learned to walk and to love: the whole universe is but an extension of that little town, somewhere in Transylvania, called Marmaroszighet.

Much of the universe in Wiesel's books is Sighet writ large. The life and death of this town haunts him. He is unable either "to get away from Sighet, or to find it again."

II

Death in Auschwitz and life in Sighet—these were the two overwhelming, irreconcilable realities for Elie

Wiesel when he left Buchenwald in April of 1945.
Even while he was still in the death camps Wiesel
knew that the Holocaust meant the end of life as he
had known it. Looking back on the experience of the
camps, he remembers asking, "Was this the end of
the Jewish people, or the end perhaps of the human
adventure?"

Constrained by such a devastating sense of ending, the survivor had few options. He could give in to
the night by means of suicide or despair, or he could
repress the Holocaust and resume life almost as if the
ending had not occurred. The first of these options
meant resignation, the second, self-delusion. There
were, however, at least two other options open to the
survivor: he could silently suffer the pain of the ending or he could begin again by telling the story of the
Holocaust.

In his life and in his literature, Elie Wiesel has
chosen these last two responses. When he was liber-
ated from Buchenwald, he took a vow not to speak or
write of his experiences for ten years. That, he
thought, might be

long enough to see clearly. Long enough to learn to listen to
the voices crying inside my own. Long enough to regain
possession of my memory. Long enough to unite the
language of men with the silence of the dead.

From 1945 to 1954, silence was Wiesel's response to
the cataclysm. During these years, he suffered the
pain of being at the end of an era, he rehearsed the
events he had undergone, and he endured the time
between the destruction of his old world and the creation of a new one.

Wiesel's vow of silence helps us to understand
why there is so little direct reporting of Holocaust experience in his work. *Night,* his first book, is the only
volume given over to a relation of his experiences in

the camps. In other books, there are only snatches of Holocaust testimony, for the concern of Wiesel's narrators is to find a way to live after the Holocaust. Hence his work continually frustrates the reader who is merely curious about the grotesqueries of the executioners and the agonies of the victims. About the Holocaust itself, Wiesel can be—and often is—hauntingly silent.

But Elie Wiesel took another vow in 1945, a vow to speak. Several days after the Americans arrived at Buchenwald, Wiesel looked at himself in a mirror for the first time since he had left Sighet. About that moment, he says:

I then decided that since everything changes—even the face in the mirror changes—someone must speak about that change. Someone must speak about the former face and that someone is I. . . . That's when I knew I was going to write.

Later, his task became even clearer to him:

After the war I absorbed. I absorbed not only the suffering, which was not mine alone—suffering everywhere in the camps—but I absorbed, unwittingly, perhaps unconsciously, the obsession to tell the tale, to bear witness. . . . I knew that anyone who remained alive had to become a storyteller, a messenger, had to speak up.

The events of the years from 1945 to 1954 are crucial for understanding how Wiesel came to write. He refused to return to Sighet after his liberation from Buchenwald, for nothing remained for him there. With several hundred other children survivors of Buchenwald, Wiesel arrived in Normandy in the summer of 1945. There began the slow process of rejoining the living, a process never to be fully completed. No longer belonging to Hungary and not a citizen of France, Wiesel was for several years a

displaced refugee, confused about place and identity.
Years later, in *A Beggar in Jerusalem* (1968), one of
Wiesel's characters remembers those days in France:

Survivors we were, but we were allowed no victory. Fear
followed us everywhere, fear preceded us. Fear of speaking
up, fear of keeping quiet. Fear of opening our eyes, fear of
shutting them. Fear of loving and being rejected or loved for
the wrong reasons, or for no reason at all. Marked, possessed, we were neither fully alive nor fully dead. People
didn't know how to handle us. We rejected charity. Pity
filled us with disgust. We were beggars, unwanted everywhere, condemned to exile and reminding strangers
everywhere of what they had done to us and to themselves.
No wonder then that in time they came to reproach us for
their own troubled consciences.

One gleam of light in this bleakness was a new
language. During the first months in Normandy and
later in Paris, which was his home base for about ten
years, Wiesel learned French. The act of learning the
language gave him a ritual that served to hold at bay
the confusion and disorder that had burst over his
world. He goes further in explaining why he chose to
learn to speak and later write in French:

Why I chose French, I don't know; maybe because it was
harder. I'm sure that symbolically it meant something to
me: it meant a new home. The language became a haven, a
new beginning, a new possibility, a new world. To start ex-
pressing myself in a new language was a defiance.

Defiance against whom? Against those who had
robbed him and his family of their life together,
against those who had sought to silence the Jews.
Learning a new language was a small yet important
way of recovering some power of self-determination.
Moreover, learning the language opened up new personal relationships, most prominently with a young
philosopher named François Wahl. In the early

months after the war, Wahl helped Wiesel learn
French and introduced him to serious philosophic
texts. In turn, Wiesel spoke of Judaism to Wahl.

The horizons of Wiesel's personal community had
contracted during the Holocaust, but the intellectual
horizons of his world expanded immensely after it.
Though he prayed less confidently than he had before
the war, he studied as resolutely. And he studied
differently. No longer was he attempting to master
doctrines that he believed implicitly. Now he was pas-
sionately questioning for himself, attempting almost
desperately to understand how the Holocaust had
been possible. He argued with God and he challenged
man, inquiring as if his life and world meaning
depended on the outcome of his inquiry.

From 1948 to 1951, Wiesel studied literature,
psychology, and philosophy at the Sorbonne. "All I
wanted," he says, "was to study," and "in a very
autodidactic manner." He wrote a dissertation com-
paring ascetic practices in the Jewish, Christian, and
Hindu traditions. For his later development, however, the most crucial influences came from the work
of the existentialists, such as Jean-Paul Sartre and
Albert Camus, who were gathering attention in the
cafés of Paris in the postwar period. The novels of
Camus—especially *The Plague*—and of André Mal-
raux—especially *Man's Fate*—were among those that
were of special importance to Wiesel. The works of
Franz Kafka and Fyodor Dostoevski also made an
impact. Later, Wiesel encountered the writings of
Martin Buber, the Jewish thinker, who, through his
interpretation of the Hasidic tradition and his
"I-Thou" philosophy, became the determining influence on Wiesel's thinking. More accurately stated,
perhaps, the ideas that combined to produce Martin
Buber's philosophy—Judaism, especially Hasidism,
and existentialism—similarly influenced Elie Wiesel.

For a number of years after the war, until the early 1960s, Wiesel worked as a journalist. He was employed for several years as a correspondent for an Israeli newspaper, first in Paris, and later in New York, where he covered the United Nations. He was able to support himself with the work, and more important, he was allowed to travel extensively, to Israel, to North Africa, to South America, and finally to the United States, where he has lived since 1956.

For ten years Wiesel kept his silence about the Holocaust, a silence made poignant because he was under a conflicting vow to speak. These were, as Wiesel has said, "ten years of preparation and reflection," during which he waited and listened. Two lines from Rainer Maria Rilke express what went on within him:

> And all was silent, yet even in the silence,
> New beginning, beckoning, change went on.[4]

In 1954, during the last year of his self-imposed silence, Wiesel's life took a crucial turn. He was working in Paris as the foreign correspondent for the Israeli newspaper *Yediot Aharonot*. As a part of an assignment, he met François Mauriac, the distinguished Catholic novelist and moral spokesman. In the course of their first conversation, Mauriac spoke of connections among Jews and Christians, and he began to praise the suffering Christ. Finally, Wiesel could bear no more, even from the irreproachable Mauriac. Rising in anger, he spoke:

I want you to know that ten years ago, not very far from here, I knew Jewish children every one of whom suffered a thousand times more, six million times more, than Christ on the cross. And we don't speak about them. Can you understand that, sir? We don't speak about them.

A friendship between Wiesel and Mauriac developed from this dramatic—for Wiesel, this central—confrontation. The old novelist implored Wiesel to write, saying: "You are wrong not to speak. . . . Listen to the old man that I am: one must speak out—one must *also* speak out." One year later, in 1955, Wiesel sent Mauriac the manuscript of *Night*, "written under the seal of memory and silence."

Wiesel's first account of the Holocaust was written in Yiddish, because he felt he owed a debt to the language and to those who spoke it. This book was published in Buenos Aires in 1956, with the title *Un di Velt Hot Geshvign (And the World Has Remained Silent)*. In 1958, a much shortened form appeared in Paris as *La Nuit* with a preface by Mauriac, who had helped Wiesel find a publisher.

The writing career—it is less a career than a mission—of Elie Wiesel was thus launched after three crucial and decisive life experiences. The first occurred in Sighet where he awoke to explore, to embody, and to celebrate the world given to him by birth. That world was not for him to create but to inhabit. The second experience, the Holocaust, was a destructive reversal that undermined and challenged all that had come before. It separated him from the world he had comfortably and assuredly inhabited. The third experience required that Wiesel begin again, this time to invent or discover a world for himself. His task involved testing the riches of the world of Sighet against the horror of the antiworld of Auschwitz. Could anything of the old world, he asked, remain after the night of the Holocaust? What resources, unknown or unexplored, could sustain a person in the post-Holocaust period?

These three experiences continue to influence the work of Elie Wiesel. While the second is the turning

14   Elie Wiesel

point and does, at least in an initial reading, dominate
his literary landscape, the first and third give
Wiesel's stories their abiding power. The Holocaust
compels Wiesel to write, but it is not the subject of his
writing. He explores the riches of the past in relation
to the questions the Holocaust raises in an effort
to articulate a meaningful way to live after the
Holocaust.

III

Since 1955, Wiesel has written incessantly. He
started with three novellas: *Night* (1958), *Dawn*
(1960), and *The Accident* (1961). The first of these is
an autobiographical treatment of his experiences in
the death camps. In the other two, the protagonists
attempt, largely unsuccessfully, to push on and find a
new post-Holocaust world in which to exist. After
writing these brief stories, Weisel expanded his narrative scope and produced four long novels: *The Town
Beyond the Wall* (1962), *The Gates of the Forest* (1964),
A Beggar in Jerusalem (1968), and *The Oath* (1973).
In these seven narratives we find the development of
Wiesel's vision. It is on these that the present study
concentrates.

    While Elie Wiesel is best known for his long nar-
rative prose, he has written in a variety of other
genres as well. There are two dramas: *Zalmen, or the
Madness of God* (1968), and *The Trial of God* (1979).
Wiesel received wide attention when *Zalmen* was
aired on national public television in 1974 after it had
first appeared in this country at the Arena Stage in
Washington, D.C. In recent years, Wiesel has taken
up the Biblical, Midrashic, and Hasidic materials that
have fascinated him since childhood. He gives a series
of interpretations in *Souls on Fire* (1972), *Four*

Hasidic Masters (1978), and *Messengers of God* (1976). For crispness and clarity of style, Wiesel is never better than in some of his shorter pieces. These have been collected in *One Generation After* (1970), *Legends of Our Time* (1966), and *A Jew Today* (1979). In 1965, after a trip to the U.S.S.R., Wiesel wrote several newspaper articles on the status of Jews there. These were later collected and published under the title *The Jews of Silence* (1966). Wiesel has also written a long dramatic poem, *Ani Maamin* (1974), set to a cantata composed by Darius Milhaud and first performed at Carnegie Hall in November, 1973.

Wiesel is perhaps as well known as a teacher and lecturer as he is as a writer. The same qualities that are present in his books are apparent in his speaking. As a lecturer, he is powerful, charismatic, sometimes overwhelmingly sad, sometimes frighteningly angry. In addition to traveling extensively to lecture, Wiesel has since 1972 held teaching posts, first at City College in New York City and later at Boston University.

In his speaking and writing, Wiesel is obsessed with the act of bearing witness. He writes:

The fear of forgetting: the main obsession of all those who have passed through the universe of the damned. The enemy counted on people's disbelief and forgetfulness. How could one foil this plot?

Wiesel attempts to foil the plot by returning from the land of the dead to become a witness; he writes "to force man to look" at what happened during the Holocaust.

But Wiesel is a visionary as well as a witness. His task is "to communicate visions that other people cannot have or cannot express." As witness, Wiesel draws on the powers of memory and expresses a loyalty to what has been; as visionary, he employs his powers of imagination to build an alternative world

and to explore what might be. With each narrative, he asks, "What would life be like if thus-and-so were the case?" In a profound way, he is dreaming his own life forward.

Elie Wiesel's life is integrally connected with his literature. At points, the stories are autobiographical in the usual sense of retrospectively rendering life in language, but they are autobiographical prospectively as well. In his stories, Wiesel goes out ahead of his actual life; he projects how it might be to experience the world in a certain way. He hypothesizes alternatives and imagines possibilities. And in several instances he has realized in his life events that occur first in his stories. The protagonist of *The Town Beyond the Wall*, for example, returns to his hometown in Hungary some twenty years after the Holocaust. Soon after writing the novel, Wiesel himself returned to Sighet. The same character imagines himself marrying and having a child. Several years later, Wiesel realized this possibility in his own life.

The work of Elie Wiesel, as much as that of any major writer at work today, exerts the healing force of the personal life history of the storyteller. Wiesel's stories record the creation of a self through memory, imagination, and moral judgment; they portray the life of feeling, the movement of thought, the deliberation of conscience. Out of his work speaks a person who has returned from a hell on earth to tell the story to an age that is impoverished, perhaps beyond recovery, by terrible and deadly violations of the human spirit.

2

....

The Journey into Night

I

Elie Wiesel has commented that *Night* is "the foundation" of his work: "All the rest is commentary." To
understand this remark, we must look first at *Night*
itself and then at the place it holds in relation to
Wiesel's other narratives. One is reluctant to apply
the usual conventions of literary analysis to the book,
for by doing so one runs the risk of blunting the impact of its testimony by too quickly speaking of sec-
ondary matters. Against the horror of the story,
literary considerations seem somehow beside the
point. And in a real sense they are, for Wiesel's principal concern is not literary. Yet he did make
authorial decisions that contribute to making *Night*
the witness that it is.

Night is autobiographical; indeed, Wiesel has said
that the story should be read in view of this statement: "I swear that every word is true." But there is
a difference between Eliezer of the book and Elie
Wiesel the storyteller. The reader's clue to this is the
difference in names: the character in the story is
"Eliezer," while the storyteller uses the name
"Elie."[1] The difference in names relates to Wiesel's
recognition that he cannot adequately convey what
happened to him and to millions of others. There
would inevitably be discrepancies between the story
he would tell and the events he suffered. It is more

truthful for him to acknowledge this by creating a slight distance between himself and his "character." With this distance, Wiesel emphasizes that a degree of the horror of the events described must remain unspoken. While *Night* is as close as Wiesel can come to the truth of his experience, it still fails to tell the whole story. "The story itself," he says, "will never be told. . . ."

The issue implicit in this discussion of *Night* is the relationship between reality and imagination. Wiesel has said:

The real and the imagined, one like the other, are part of history; one is its shell, the other its core. Not to recognize this is to deny art—any form of art—the right to exist.

This comment suggests that, as a historical account, *Night* is comprised of both the real and the imagined. The real—that is, Wiesel's actual life experience—provides the content; the imagination—his powers as storyteller—provides the form. A story about one's life, for him, does not aim to provide bare facts: facts must be placed in a context, the relationship existing among disparate items of information must be established. For Wiesel, the storyteller's task is, through imagination, to shape experience in such a way that the deepest truth of his life will be disclosed.

Wiesel's understanding of his own creative process as a storyteller, then, warrants us to inquire about how his imagination worked in shaping *Night*. The book reflects the results of ten years of remembering. It represents reality distilled through a well-conceived and powerfully executed form. To understand fully what Wiesel is saying about the Holocaust, we must look closely at the way he tells the story.

One of the most striking features of *Night* is Wiesel's control of the language. In the manner of

reportage, the language describes the events directly, without polemic, without extensive intervention by the narrator, and without self-pity. The language is sparse, taut, and concise. The events are allowed to speak for themselves. The writing perhaps requires such control because the reality about which it speaks is so uncontrolled, so savage, and so thorough in its malevolence. The narrator's tone displays the same evenness and terseness, changing only infrequently to allow naked anger or horror to break through. The tone, moreover, is nonaccusatory. It is hauntingly sad. Irony is sometimes present, but it is not a bitter or strident or revengeful irony. The irony of *Night* makes the sadness more poignant, for it arises not from the narrator's cleverness but from painful discrepancies between his (and the reader's) expectations and the events he narrates.

Night tells what Eliezer underwent from the end of 1941 to April, 1945. To give form to the events Wiesel employs two familiar framing devices: those of a story or initiation and a story of journey. Inside these loose frames, Wiesel arranges the vignettes so that the story reads like a simple chronicle of Eliezer's experience. In order not to violate the experience he is relating, Wiesel refrains from imposing too severe an order on what was essentially an eruption of disorder in his world.

As an initiation story, the narrative explores the way in which a boy in his early teens goes through difficult trials to discover something new about himself, his people, and the world in which he is to live. Early in the story, the narrator suggests the importance of "initiation." The initiation to which he refers is conducted by Mochè, Eliezer's teacher in the mysteries of the Kabbala and other secret matters of Jewish thought. Given the multitude of possible starting points for the story, it is crucial that Wiesel chose to

open with Mochè. The opening suggests that Wiesel wants us to read the story in the light of this picture of Eliezer as a religious seeker. What happens subsequently largely takes its meaning from the contrast between the experience of the Holocaust and Eliezer's early religious intensity.

This opening accentuates the initiation motif as well. The initiation to which the narrator refers involves a religious master and an earnest seeker. The master presumably knows something that the disciple does not; he is in touch with a hidden truth that can be discerned only after a long quest. Mochè introduces Eliezer to the *Zohar*, the Book of Splendor, a mystical commentary on the first books of the Bible. As a Kabbalist, Mochè is concerned with directing his student's soul toward the long, arduous ascent of the ladder of mystical enlightenment to a final disclosure of and union with the Eternal God. With the war, everything changes for the boy, but the change occurs downward toward darkness and nothingness. His initiation ends in despair and chaos, not hope and order; in isolation and horror, not in a community sustained by joy.

Under the tutelage of Mochè, Eliezer had set out on a path leading to life. Instead, he enters into death, which takes over his existence. Death is everywhere in the camps: in the chimneys and fences, in the faces of the executioners, and in the eyes of the prisoners. Death floats in the clouds as the smoke from the chimneys slowly rises day after day. "Around me," Eliezer says, "everything was dancing a dance of death. It made my head reel. I was walking in a cemetery, among stiffened corpses, logs of wood." Silently but perceptibly, death enters the soul of Eliezer, and although he escapes physical death, he comes to belong more to the dead than to the living. At the end of the narrative, Eliezer looks at himself:

"From the depths of the mirror, a corpse gazed back at me. The look in his eyes, as they stared into mine, has never left me."

The motif of initiation in *Night* is closely associated with the motif of journey. Before the Holocaust, Eliezer had set out on a spiritual journey whose destination was union with God. He had hoped that Mochè would draw him "into eternity," away from the vicissitudes of bodily existence in time. Again, Eliezer's expectations are radically reversed, for he is forced into the worst of physical journeys. It begins with the ride in the cattle train to Auschwitz. After three weeks there, he walks to Buna, where he remains until January, 1945. During that time, the prisoners are marched to work outside the camp every day. In January, 1945, there is a savage march in the snow to Gleiwitz, followed closely by a ten-day ride in an open cattle car to Buchenwald. All the while, the young boy increasingly becomes obsessed with physical survival. Instead of a disclosure of divine mystery at the end of this journey, there is the death of God and a revelation of absolute evil at the heart of things. Instead of being transported out of the body and into the bliss of eternity, Eliezer moves steadily into degradation in an agonized physical world.

Lawrence Cunningham has noticed that the journey in *Night* reverses at many points the Biblical story of the Exodus.[2] For example, in the Bible the Angel of Death passes over and gives special protection to Hebrew children. In *Night*, Jewish children are marked first for death. The ancient story speaks of a pillar of fire that leads the people by night and a cloud of smoke that guides them by day. In the kingdom of night, the pillars of fire and smoke come from the crematories at Auschwitz. In the Biblical narrative, the God elects the Hebrews to a special status; at

Auschwitz there is the ominous "selection" in which
Jews are chosen to die. The Hebrews of the Bible
enter into a covenant with their God and are promised a long life if they obey the divine commandments.
In Eliezer's experience, only Hitler keeps his promises, and religious observances become irrelevant and
even harmful. Indeed, survival in the camps entails
the deliberate breaking of ritual injunctions. To fast
on holy days hastens one's death by starvation; to tell
the truth shortens one's life.

The change in his journey from a spiritual odys-
sey to a physical one is accompanied by a shift in
Eliezer's stance on religious matters. At the beginning of the story, Eliezer takes the mysteries of the
Kabbala to be the key to what is ultimately real. Later
he speaks of "cabbalistic dreams." Earlier the holy
days were the grandest days; later he views Yom
Kippur as a "mirage." Eliezer radically questions
religious beliefs, in part because he fears that the
beliefs themselves contribute to the prisoners'
destruction. Some victims submit willingly to the executioner because they see submission almost as a
religious obligation.

But Eliezer's journey has spiritual dimensions as
well. His spirit moves downward in an ever narrowing spiral. The first and last words of the English
version of the book reflect one dimension of the con-
tracting movement of the whole. The English version
opens with the word "they" and ends with the word
"me." "They" refers to the Jewish community in
which Eliezer had lived. That community and the
town of which it was a part linked him to the cosmos
and to all of history. Its rituals and holy days imbued
the passing of time with order and majesty. The
world of that community was rich in stories,
memories, and hopes for time and eternity.

Eliezer's movement into the night represents a

gradual and seemingly inevitable contraction of this earlier world as one after another of its elements are stripped away. First the larger world of the town contracts into a ghetto, and then, it is left behind. Along the way, the religious community is destroyed, God absents Himself, the family is shattered. With the death of Eliezer's father, the spiraling down into the narrowing chasm is complete, and Eliezer is left "terribly alone in a world without God and without man." The journey is at its end.

II

If we are fully to understand how *Night* is the foundation of Wiesel's work and to build an adequate foundation with which to read the remainder of his narratives, we must look at several components of the story besides the journey and initiation motifs. Above all, Wiesel is concerned with relationships. In speaking of the meaning of the Holocaust, he emphasizes this: "Something happened a generation ago, to the world, to man. Something happened to God. Certainly something happened to the relations between man and God, man and man, man and himself."

Night records how the Holocaust poisoned and nearly destroyed all primary relationships in Eliezer's life. His relationship to himself—and by this is meant his understanding of himself—is called into question on the first night at Auschwitz. He says:

The student of the Talmud, the child I was, had been consumed in the flames. There remained only a shape that looked like me. A dark flame had entered into my soul and devoured it.

Eliezer's sense of himself as a pious Jewish youth jars

with his situation in the death camp: nothing in his previous identity could prepare him for this confrontation with absolute evil. Faced with this discrepancy between his situation and his understanding of himself, Eliezer no longer knows who he is or what he has to do.

His relationship to God is similarly disrupted. Immediately, Job-like, Eliezer begins to question the justice of God. How could God allow good people to suffer so? In accord with the pattern of reversals we noted earlier, Eliezer reverses the place of man and God. When, for example, the Jews assemble to pray on Rosh Hashanah, he comments: "This day I had ceased to plead. I was no longer capable of lamentation. On the contrary, I felt very strong. I was the accuser, God the accused." In much Jewish theology of suffering, God places the Jews on trial either as punishment for sin or as a way of further purifying the chosen people for their redemptive task. In *Night*, the relationship between God and man is first questioned and then reversed: God becomes the guilty one who has transgressed and who deserves to be on trial. God, not man, has broken His promises and betrayed His people.

While his relationships to himself and to God are crucial for Eliezer, his relationship to his father is important as well. Through much of his time in the death camps this relationship remains the single tie to his life in Sighet. Just as Eliezer's relationship with God is the center of the religious dimension of the story, his relationship with his father is the center of the psychological quandary. To Wiesel, the two relationships are intrinsically connected, but they are not reducible to each other. They are distinct, each with its own integrity and its own significance. Both add focus to Eliezer's identity, so that the loss of either is

psychically disturbing, and the loss of both altogether devastating.

The tenacity with which Eliezer clings to his father reflects an effort to draw back from the abyss that opens up with the loss of all human ties. The relationship functions as a touchstone to which Eliezer (and the entire narrative) returns again and again. He measures what is happening within himself in terms of what is happening in his relationship with his father. If he can sustain his unconditional commitment to his father, then something might abide in a world in which all is changing. Since anything can suddenly be taken away from the inmates of the death camps, Eliezer makes only one thing necessary to him: absolute fidelity to his father. God has broken His promises to His people; Eliezer, in contrast, determines ever more resolutely not to violate his covenant with his father.

Eliezer's struggle to maintain decency in his principal relationships finally focuses on this question: Will he betray his father and choose his own life at his father's expense? Eliezer watches one young man kill his father for a piece of bread; he sees another, Rabbi Eliahou's son, run off and leave his father in the snow. Gathering the last particles of outrage he possesses, Eliezer prays to a God whom he no longer trusts: "My God, Lord of the Universe, give me strength never to do what Rabbi Eliahou's son has done."

After the long journey to Buchenwald, Eliezer's complex relationship to his father reaches its culmination. Seeing that Eliezer's struggle to keep his father alive is depleting his meager energy, the head of the block counsels him:

Listen to me, boy. Don't forget that you're in a concentration camp. Here, every man has to fight for himself and not

think of anyone else. Even of his father. Here, there are no
fathers, no brothers, no friends. Everyone lives and dies for
himself alone.

In response, Eliezer reflects: "He was right, I
thought in the most secret region of my heart, but I
dared not admit it." Eliezer continues to struggle
against what he considers to be the final debasement
of his humanity: to choose himself over his father. But
when his father dies, Eliezer makes this disturbing
admission:

And, in the depths of my being, in the recesses of my
weakened conscience, could I have searched it, I might
perhaps have found something like—free at last!

With this event the concentration camp has
worked its horror completely in the boy's soul. In his
view, he is guilty of having acquiesced in his father's
death. The reader is likely to pity Eliezer, but Eliezer
asks for no sympathy. In disclosing his feelings,
Eliezer simply confesses the extent to which the
Holocaust has corrupted the primary relationships of
life. In stripping away a person's past, in pushing him
to the limits of his physical endurance, in reversing all
the expectations he had of man and God—in all these
ways life in the camps forced the victim to choose
himself without regard for the other. "At that moment," Eliezer sadly admits, "what did the others
matter!"

Here Wiesel displays the effect of suffering on
the soul of the victim. He refuses to sentimentalize or
legitimate undeserved suffering by bestowing on it
some healing or expiatory power or by pretending
that suffering of itself ennobles the human spirit.
People respond differently to suffering: some hold in-
tact their previous world views, some become angry
and finally despair, some transform suffering into an
occasion for compassion toward the self and others,

some become bitter and resentful. Wiesel shows that the suffering caused by the Holocaust, which certainly exceeded what human beings are normally asked to endure, evoked all these responses among the victims. He seems, however, most deeply troubled by the way in which suffering distorts a person. The protagonists of *The Accident* insists that

Suffering brings out the lowest, the most cowardly in man. There is a phase of suffering you reach beyond which you become a brute: beyond it you sell your soul—and worse, the souls of your friends—for a piece of bread, for some warmth, for a moment of oblivion, of sleep.

Those who undergo such suffering "no longer dare look at themselves in the mirror, afraid they may see their inner image: a monster . . . ."

For Elie Wiesel, victimization carried far enough and imposed brutally enough finally so distorts a person that he becomes unrecognizable even to himself. The victimization that occurred in the Holocaust revealed to Wiesel a capacity within the human soul that he could not have imagined during the days of his childhood in Sighet. An initial shock takes over Eliezer's soul when he sees that the Germans and his fellow Hungarians can be monstrous in their relationships to the Jews; a more unsettling disclosure is that God Himself can betray His people; but the final and perhaps most devastating shock arises from the disclosure that Eliezer himself is capable of disregard for his own father. The insight that no relationship is immune to the eruption of evil: this is what the experience of the Holocaust discloses to Wiesel.

III

In many ways, *Night* ends with the death of Eliezer's

father and the anguished admission, "free at last!"
Although Eliezer remains in Buchenwald for four
more months, the narrative comes quickly to a close.
In the final pages, the tone of the writing changes
slightly: it becomes more reportorial, as though the
narrator were speaking about someone else.

Until the death of his father, Eliezer fights the
forces set against him, but afterwards, he becomes
more resigned to whatever fate may be his. Fundamental to the Judaism of his childhood was a belief
that what happened to him was a part of God's provi-
dential care. Events did not occur randomly: rather,
God guided history toward a glorious end. But the
concentration camp calls into question the Jewish
idea of history. For Eliezer, the magnitude of
undeserved suffering renders the notion of God's control over history questionable if not morally repug-
nant. Eliezer begins to see that the interior of the
self—who he is, what he values, what he decides—has
no significant effect on the course of external events.
There is no connection between who he is and what
happens to him; there is no connection between what
he does and what he receives from life. Human
agency has little if any meaning in this moral context;
action loses credibility as an indicator of character.

During his final months in the camps, the scope
of Eliezer's world shrinks. He comments:

I have nothing to say of my life during this period. It no
longer mattered. After my father's death, nothing could
touch me any more. . . . I had but one desire—to eat. I no
longer thought of my father or of my mother.

Night reminds us that there are some simple and
ordinary elements of human existence—food, trust,
conversation, and, as a context for all things, human
relationships—without which the spirit withers. De-

prived of these things, the self can hardly expect to find significance in life.

About his last months in the camps, Eliezer has "nothing to say." Having nothing to say of one's life means that it is not worthy of being rendered as a story. The richer the life, the more complex its struggles, and the sharper and more intense its conflicts, the more compelling is the impulse to make stories. Eliezer's life no longer deserves comment. This storylessness becomes more revealing when we recall that the world in which Eliezer lived prior to the Holocaust was wonderfully filled with stories. There were the grand legends of Biblical heroes, the tales about Hasidic masters and their miracles, and the stories of the family. Life was replete with stories: all things mattered and were worthy of being molded into story. The life of the individual and of the community was guided by stories, and the panorama of history was elucidated by the Jewish story of redemption.

When Eliezer is left with no story to tell, the Nazis are victorious, for the Nazis sought to kill all the Jewish stories. They knew that if the continuity of memory could be severed the life of the Jewish community would be gone. And during the last months in the camp, that intent is realized in Eliezer's life. He becomes a storyless cipher, with no one to talk to and nothing of importance to say. He has, in effect, forgotten everything.

IV

Night is the foundation of Wiesel's work because it records the way in which the Holocaust brought the world of Sighet to an end. The story records the

crucial turning point in Wiesel's personal life history and in his understanding of the history of humankind, and it marks the place from which he begins his work as a writer.

The book, however, is a foundation in another unexpected way. While *Night* records a story of destruction, it contains hints of other stories. Over the years, as he moved from book to book, Wiesel developed possibilities that are mentioned, but that are hidden or only partially portrayed, in *Night*. About this process, Wiesel is explicit:

Night, my first narrative, was an autobiographical story, a kind of testimony of one witness speaking of his own life, his own death. All kinds of options were available: suicide, madness, killing, political action, hate, friendship. I note all of these options [in *Night*] . . . and in each book I explore one aspect. In *Dawn*, I explore the political action; in *The Accident*, I explore suicide; in *The Town Beyond the Wall*, madness; in *A Beggar in Jerusalem*, history, the return. All the stories are one story, except that I build them in concentric circles. The center is the same and it is in *Night*. What happened during that night I'm afraid will not be revealed.

Wiesel himself speaks of concentric circles of which *Night* is the center, and we might also see his development as a spiral. *Night* follows the pattern of a spiral as the contours of Eliezer's world become smaller and smaller. Wiesel's development as a writer reverses the process. Each narrative returns to the center in *Night* to evoke the experience of the Holocaust; it then moves outward to encompass a wider range of human experience. And with each succeeding narrative, greater expanses of time and richer meanings are encompassed. This process is repeated with every book, and this is one reason why we find considerable overlap among Wiesel's narratives. We sometimes have the sense of reading the

same story again and again as we move from novel to novel. And in a profound sense we are, for Wiesel goes over the same or almost the same path repeatedly. But with every return to and movement out from the center of *Night*, he sees more and goes farther, always seeking to disclose aspects of human experience not yet adequately explored.

The spirallike movement of Wiesel's sensibility is implicit in the pattern of reversals that we have already noted. *Night* is a story of reversal; it shows how the world that Eliezer had known in Sighet was turned upside down and inside out. The world of the Holocaust is to the world of Sighet as a negative is to a photographic print: the image is reversed, and a ghastly half-light is cast over the scene. *Night* shows how what Wiesel calls the "philosophy of the concentration camp" took over. That philosophy meant "every man for himself, every man the enemy of the next man, for each lived at the other's expense"; it meant "above all, no initiative . . . ." In the concentration camps, "it is the strongest and the most brutal who is in the right"; the prisoners "dreaded disturbances, surprises."

Wiesel's subsequent work reverses the experience of *Night*. It attempts to recapture life prior to the Holocaust but to do so without forgetting the Holocaust. Wiesel begins with night, but he moves through to day; he begins in despair and silence, but moves to hope and speech; he begins with the absence of God, but moves to reaffirm God's presence wherever human beings encounter each other; he begins with isolation and moves to explore the meaning of friendship and human community.

It would be too simple to suggest that Elie Wiesel merely negates the negative in behalf of the positive. Rather, he explores the continuous presence of both the negative and the positive in the human soul and

the way in which they require each other's presence.) More importantly, he urges his readers to enlist their lives in behalf of the positive. Storytelling, for Wiesel, is part of the battle against the forces of darkness and death, evil and despair. During the Holocaust, he actually and literally fought against these forces; through storytelling, he continues to fight. "I try to fight the killers," he says, "through re-creating the world they tried to destroy." And he hopes that the reader will so imaginatively encounter the forces of darkness in the stories as to be moved to fight them in real life.

It is true that Wiesel comes to reject despair and death in favor of hope and life, but it is also true that the Holocaust remains ever with him. He reaffirms some of life's satisfactions and some of the aspirations that he had as a child in Sighet, but he also returns again and again to the agony of Auschwitz. It is an agony that abides: this is the foundation of Elie Wiesel's life and work.

3

....

The Drama of Interrogation

Some writers are advocates. They possess a clarity of vision that makes an assertive tone natural and comfortable to them. Other writers are more at ease with the exclamatory tone. Excitement and celebration of the world punctuates their work. Yet as necessary as assertion and exclamation are, without interrogation our declarations sound hollow and our exclamations inauthentic.

Elie Wiesel characteristically maintains an interrogatory attitude toward the mysteries of existence, both human and divine. He ventures to make assertions, which emerge out of a struggle with both despair and hope; he also risks exclamations, which express delight in the everyday. Yet in its subject matter and in its fundamental vision of life, his work reflects that "the essence of man is to be a question, and the essence of the question is to be without answer."

With *Night* the interrogative process that extends throughout Wiesel's work begins. From his first night in Auschwitz, Eliezer questions. Wiesel is careful, however, to point out that questions were also a part of pre-Holocaust life. Indeed, when Mochè first speaks in *Night*, he asks Eliezer: "Why do you weep when you pray? . . . Why do you pray?" On his

33

first day with Mochè, which parallels his first night in
Auschwitz, Eliezer learns that:

Man raises himself toward God by the questions he asks
Him . . . . That is the true dialogue. Man questions God and
God answers. But we don't understand His answers. We
can't understand them. Because they come from the depths
of the soul, and they stay there until death.

Mochè's words are puzzling, for Judaism seems
at first glance to consist of answers, not of questions.
The Biblical Mochè (Moses) did not deliver a set of
questions to the ancient Hebrews: he gave them a set
of apodictic laws. The religious sentiment often
seems to be antithetical to questioning. Rabbi Israel
Meir Hacohen, a leader of East European Jewry prior
to World War II, expressed the suspicion that
religious persons often feel toward questions: "For
the believer there are no questions; and for the
unbeliever there are no answers."[1]
How then can Mochè, and Wiesel himself, engage
in questioning as though it were an expression of
religious devotion? Wiesel assigns to questioning a
determining role in the Jewish tradition. Of special
importance to him are Biblical figures, such as Job
and Jeremiah, who question the justice of God, puzzle
over the suffering of the innocent, or ponder God's
delay in fulfilling His promises. Wiesel traces his own
questioning back to that of these Biblical figures.
Similarly, he emphasizes the way in which Hasidic
masters of the eighteenth and nineteenth centuries
questioned the Messiah's failure to come and redeem
the world.[2] For Wiesel, questioning is a bridge across
the chasm the Holocaust opened in the history of the
Jews: questioning links him to the past.
Wiesel's questioning is religious in the narrow
sense that he asks about God, evil, suffering, and the
future of Judaism. But it is religious in a broader
sense as well, if by *religious* we mean "asking pas-

sionately the question of the meaning of our existence and being willing to receive answers . . . ."[3] In Wiesel's work, this type of religious questioning takes the distinctly modern shape of an inquiry into the nature of the self. "In a time of the eclipse of God," Nathan Scott has commented, "the most characteristic form of the religious question becomes the question of authenticity, of how we are to keep faith with and safeguard the 'single one' or the 'true self'—in a bullying world."[4] Such questioning about the self is a key element in Elie Wiesel's work.

Questioning consists of an interchange between question and answer. Honest questioning requires that one endeavor to formulate a response. Hence, although its principal creative impulse is that of questioning, Wiesel's work is assertive as well. It gains ethical intensity and enlarges its scope through its efforts to provide meaningful responses to painful religious, social, and psychological questions.

The spirit of questioning in itself gives no special distinction to Wiesel's works. Human beings are questioners, as almost every serious Western writer has emphasized. Questioning is not something invented in the twentieth century, even with its sordid record of atrocities and exploded dreams. What finally distinguishes Elie Wiesel is the shape his questioning takes and the significance it has for discerning a way of meaningfully dwelling in the post-Holocaust world. His questioning takes the ancient form of storytelling. It is the stories that we ourselves must question and be questioned by if the vision that orders Elie Wiesel's world is to be revealed.

I

We have already seen how, in *Night*, the Holocaust undermines Eliezer's earlier understanding of

himself, of others, and of God. We need now to turn
to Wiesel's later novels to examine more closely how
these seeming certainties become questionable for
other protagonists. For Wiesel, three questions, Who
am I? Who are You?, and Who is God? are linked
together. To ask one of these questions is to ask the
other two as well.

One of Wiesel's characters comments: "When he
opened his eyes, Adam did not ask God: 'Who are
you?' He asked: 'Who am I?' " So it is for the survivor,
who in several respects is like a new Adam: "Reduced
to a mere number, the man in the concentration camp
at the same time lost his identity and his individual
destiny." After his release from the camp, the survivor thus was compelled to embark on a path of self-
creation and self-discovery. Wiesel described this
process in three novellas. Eliezer in *Night*, Elisha in
Dawn, and Eliezer in *The Accident* are characters
without futures. They have only pasts cruelly dominated by the smoke of the Holocaust and presents
punctuated by memories of childhood lost in the
flames. For them, the "I" has curled into a question
mark.

In the manner of Job, Eliezer in *Night* seeks to
understand himself by questioning God. He questions
with haunting intensity:

What are You, my God . . . compared to this afflicted
crowd, proclaiming to You their faith, their anger, their
revolt? What does Your greatness mean, Lord of the
Universe, in the face of all this weakness, this decomposi-
tion, and this decay? Why do You still trouble their sick
minds, their crippled bodies?

Such questioning does not mean that Eliezer no
longer believes in God; indeed, he says, "I did not
doubt His existence, but I did doubt His absolute

justice." Questioning is Eliezer's way of relating to God. In *A Jew Today*, Wiesel writes: "Of course man must interrogate God, as did Abraham; articulate his anger, as did Moses; and shout his sorrow, as did Job. But only the Jews opt for Abraham—who questions—*and* for God—who is questioned."

The questions that Eliezer raises in *Night* recall the scene early in the narrative in which Mochè counsels his young disciple: "You will find the true answers, Eliezer, only within yourself." But at the end of the story, Mochè's words ring hollow against the measure of Eliezer's experience. When the Americans arrive at Buchenwald, Eliezer sees within himself only silence, apathy, aloneness, detachment, hunger. Mochè spoke of a mystical moment in which the religious devotee discovers a harmony between the deepest dimensions of his interior life and God Himself. But at the end of the story, Eliezer finds nothing of the sort. He finds a horrible nothingness within.

Night, however, does not give Wiesel's final answer to the question of self-identity. For all the outrage and suffering it portrays, *Night* is the beginning, not the ending, of Wiesel's inquiry into the nature of the self. Hence, his second book interrogates *Night*.

Dawn questions Mochè's notion that the solitary individual will find answers within himself. It moves the search for meaningful self-identity outside the individual into the realm of political action. The story discloses, however, that while the search for meaning within the self is painful and perilous, action in the political realm may be equally ambiguous.

The story's protagonist is Elisha, like Eliezer a survivor of the death camps. After the war, he goes to study philosophy at the Sorbonne, where he defines himself as a questioner:

So many questions obsessed me. Where is God to be found? In suffering or in rebellion? When is a man most truly a man? When he submits or when he refuses? Where does suffering lead him? To purification or to bestiality? Philosophy, I hoped, would give me an answer.

But as Eliezer's study of the Talmud in Sighet was interrupted by the Nazis, so is Elisha surprised by a mysterious Jew named Gad, who abruptly enters Elisha's life and demands his attention. By sheer force of personality, Gad recruits Elisha to go to Palestine and join the fight against the British for the creation of the state of Israel.

Gad is the first of a series of provocative intruders to appear in Wiesel's stories. About him, Elisha comments: "If today I am only a question mark, he is responsible." How can Elisha say this when he had already been a questioner before he met Gad? A clue to the answer is given in a second comment:

I saw in him a prince of Jewish history, a legendary messenger sent to awaken my imagination, to tell the people whose past was now their religion: Come, come; the future is waiting with open arms.

Elisha's questioning had locked him in the past. He had been repeatedly reviewing the events of the Holocaust, rehearsing the ways in which his experience had contradicted the promises God had made to the Jews. Gad breaks through these insular, circular thought processes by calling on Elisha to break out of his captivity to the past and embrace a future for himself. "Man," Wiesel has said, "cannot live indefinitely without a dream and without a legend." Yet that was what Elisha was attempting to do: he had no dream for the future, only nightmares of the past. He had no legend, no guide, no heroes, no project for his life, only a chronicle of death. Gad

awakens his imagination so that Elisha once again comes into contact with the living.

The irony of Gad's influence on Elisha is that although he awakens Elisha's imagination and thereby leads him to question the future, he at the same time circumscribes the future by insisting that Elisha follow a specific path. Instead of discovering a future for himself, Elisha borrows the future that Gad provides. Gad has a definite vision of what Jews must be and do:

We can rely only on ourselves. If we must become more unjust and inhuman than those who have been unjust and inhuman to us, then we shall do so. We don't like to be bearers of death; heretofore we've chosen to be victims rather than executioners. . . . But that's all over; we must be like everybody else.

Gad presents this answer to the problem of identity for Elisha and his people; the action of the story, however, displays how difficult it will be for Elisha to assume this new identity.

In Palestine, Elisha is faced with a cruel reversal of fate: whereas during the Holocaust he had been a victim, he is now asked to be an executioner. Appointed to kill a British officer as a reprisal for the death of a Jew, Elisha feels as if he is putting on the uniform of the SS. As the hours pass before the dawn at which he is to kill John Dawson, figures from Elisha's past haunt his consciousness. He cannot justify his action to them, for his family and his tradition stand against the taking of human life. Until now, he had maintained his tenuous hold on self-identity by attachment to his tradition. If he were to commit murder, he would no longer be an innocent victim. He would no longer be a Jew who fights death and chooses life.

When Elisha murders John Dawson at dawn, he

does not triumphantly throw off the identity of the victim and embrace that of the executioner. Rather, he says, "I've killed. I've killed Elisha." To kill is to violate or even abrogate his previous sense of himself. The Hebrew name "Elisha" means "God is salvation." The Biblical prophet by that name resuscitated a boy who had died. Hence to be Elisha is to carry the saving, lifegiving power of God. Instead of acting as an instrument of salvation, Elisha reverses the action of the prophet whose name he bears: whereas the Biblical Elisha restored a man from the dead, this Elisha murders a man.

Thus the dawn to which the title refers is an ambiguous one. We see this at the end of the story, for after the execution the ghosts from Elisha's past depart, leaving him alone. He goes to the window and sees his own face, which signals that night still remains. The clock says it is dawn, and Gad had promised the dawning of a new future if Elisha would embrace political action. But for Elisha's spirit, it is still night. Night lingers because Elisha, even as a member of a unified, activist group, remains alone. His action isolates him. He seems to feel that he has bought a future at the price of his past.

Why is being an executioner so radical a break from Elisha's tradition? A part of the answer is theological: the executioner places himself above God; he assumes sovereignty over life itself. As Elisha waits for dawn, he reflects that it is "not easy to play the part of God." Wiesel later extends these thoughts in *One Generation After*:

The executioners assumed the role of God. They alone could, by decree, proclaim the limits of good and evil. Their idiosyncrasies were law and so were their whims. They were above morality, above truth.

In Jewish tradition, since God is the source of life, to kill is to usurp God's proper place.

As the executioner exalts himself, he diminishes his victim. Armies and governments, Elisha says, justify murder by creating "an image of the enemy in which he is the incarnation of evil, the symbol of suffering, the fountainhead of the cruelty and injustice of all times." So reduced, the enemy is not seen as a complex human being. The Biblical vision of all persons being created in the "image of God" is forgotten. Elisha struggles (but finally fails) to reduce John Dawson in this way: "I mustn't listen to him, I told myself. He's my enemy, and the enemy has no story." To have a story is to be a complex person with hopes and fears, commitments and affections, memories and hopes. The executioner, Wiesel suggests, must refuse to allow his victim such complexity, or else murder will be difficult or impossible. In short, the executioner must question neither who the victim is nor what the murder means.

While the theological implications of murder are important, another factor makes the execution problematic for Elisha as well. He senses that both he and Dawson are trapped by a situation they did not create:

The fear of either the victim or the executioner is unimportant. What matters is the fact that each of them is playing a role which has been imposed upon him. The two roles are the extremities of the estate of man. The tragic thing is the imposition.

Because he is playing a role, Elisha cannot justify his action to himself. Were he to hate Dawson, his action would acquire "a meaning which may somehow transcend it," for "hate justifies everything." But Elisha rather likes Dawson, and he realizes that "under other circumstances" the two might have been friends. Thus on a personal level the murder is a tragic act, if not an absurd one, because there is a disjunction between Elisha's feeling and his action;

there is a discrepancy between his deepest sense of himself and the role he is expected to play. Whereas the Nazis had robbed Elisha of his selfhood in the Holocaust, he now gives his selfhood away by performing an action that contradicts both his past and his deepest feelings for life.

What message does Wiesel intend Elisha to convey? That Gad is wrong in suggesting that the Jews must become like everybody else? That murder, even in behalf of an important political effort, can never be justified? That all men, Jews as well as Nazis, will become executioners under certain circumstances? That political action *as such* is contradictory to a satisfying sense of personal identity?

Wiesel does not fully resolve these questions in this brief narrative, but he does give clues to the lines of inquiry that he develops more fully in later books. First, Wiesel does not palliate the Nazis' guilt by suggesting that all persons will commit murder in compelling circumstances. The truth is that not all persons commit murder, much less participate in genocidal madness on the scale of the Nazis. The Nazis, furthermore, would be no less guilty because other persons, even Jews, were to become executioners.

Second, Wiesel finally disagrees with Gad's suggestion that Jews "must be like everybody else." *Dawn* does suggest the necessity for rebellion against victimization rather than passive acceptance of the victim's role. But for Wiesel, to become like "everybody else" would be to reject the past and to dishonor the victims of the Holocaust. If Jews must kill, Wiesel implies, they must kill reluctantly, with regret and anguish.

Dawn's importance lies in what it reveals about the creation and discovery of a meaningful self-identity. Wiesel suggests that in acting in behalf of the future every person necessarily pays the price of

his innocence. Elisha loses his innocence whether he goes through with the murder or refuses. This fact does not justify his act; rather, it reminds us that human action is necessarily ambiguous. Perhaps killing Dawson is Elisha's most satisfactory choice, yet he still must face the consequences of his action. He does so by anticipating the grief of Dawson's widow and son and by realizing that the murder violates his religious tradition.

Wiesel suggests that action inevitably leaves its mark on the actor. Elisha cannot commit murder and expect to remain unscathed by it. We become what we do, as Elisha realizes:

There are not a thousand ways of being a killer; either a man is one or he isn't. He can't say I'll kill only ten or only five minutes or a single day. He who has killed one man alone is a killer for life.

Such a naked statement of a complex moral issue jars the reader. We are accustomed to moral relativism, and we sometimes hear that because a person kills he is not thereby a killer—he may be a good and decent person who merely deviates from his habitual pattern of actions. Elisha (and Wiesel) would not allow such a softening of the moral vision, for to do so would open the door to excusing the Nazi officers who played their roles, obeyed their orders, and murdered thousands of people, maintaining all the while that they were essentially innocent, decent folk.

Dawn explores the ethical and religious complexity of Elisha's choosing a future. A clue to this is given in the prologue to the narrative. Elisha speaks: " 'Tomorrow I shall kill a man,' I said to myself, reeling in my fall." For Wiesel, it seems that to act is to fall, in an ethical and religious sense. *Dawn* is the story of a fall: it recapitulates the fall of Adam, or more accurately, the fall of Cain. In the Bible, Cain

kills his brother Abel. In Wiesel's narrative, Elisha follows in this path by killing John Dawson; like Cain, he usurps the place of God as the giver and taker of life.

It is perhaps odd that in Wiesel's first narrative after *Night*, a Jew commits murder and thereby loses his innocence. One would have expected the writer to turn to direct indictment of the Nazis. Wiesel, however, is less interested in writing about the Nazis than he is in imagining a way of life after their gruesome work is over. He does so by facing up to a tendency of the victims of the Holocaust. The Holocaust polluted the executioners and, in a strange way, purified the victims. Wiesel's characters, having endured such suffering, are tempted to try to be perfect. As the victim of undeserved suffering sets out to create a new world, he wishes to build a decent, even pure, world free of the brutality and betrayals of the old world.

In *Dawn* Elie Wiesel exposes the desire for purity in the new world after the Holocaust. He does not weaken his condemnation of the Nazis, but neither does he wish to pretend that a life free of wrongdoing is possible. It might be, Wiesel implies, that the victims' desire to be innocent contributed to their victimization. In *Dawn*, Wiesel suggests that if one is never again to be a victim one must relinquish the ideal and illusion of innocence. In his effort to achieve a new sense of identity in the post-Holocaust world, the survivor will be unable to avoid the ambiguous nature of all human action. One must be willing to fall.

III

The process of questioning that begins in *Night* and

Dawn continues in *The Accident* (the title of which is an unfortunate translation of *Le Jour*—"day"). In many ways this is the bitterest of Elie Wiesel's books. The protagonist, once again called Eliezer, carries the legacy of the Holocaust:

At first I had had a hard time getting used to the idea that I was alive. I thought of myself as dead. I couldn't eat, read, cry: I saw myself dead. I thought I was dead and that in a dream I imagined myself alive. I knew I no longer existed, that my real self had stayed *there*, that my present self had nothing in common with the other, the real one. I was like the skin shed by a snake.

Although these words describe Eliezer immediately following his release from the death camp, they accurately portray his plight ten years later when the action of the novel occurs. He still questions his identity: "You want to know who I am, truly? I don't know myself."

In the years since the war, Wiesel's protagonist apparently has made little progress in moving beyond the Holocaust experience. We see here the spirallike character of Wiesel's work, as mentioned in a previous chapter. With every book, Wiesel returns to his starting place, as if seeking in the origin of things some secret to assist with the new situation. His protagonists begin at the same point and repeat the same process, but with each successive novel the protagonist moves farther forward toward significant identity than the earlier protagonists did. This repetition emphasizes that, for Wiesel, the journey the self takes is not one directional: it is a process in which one repeatedly recoils to the past in order better to engage the present time.

The Accident is the story of Eliezer's recovery from the "accident" of being struck by a taxi in New York. Just as he had survived the Holocaust some ten

years earlier, he is again miraculously saved, in large part because of the efforts of a surgeon named Paul Russell. The relationship between Eliezer and Russell, however, is more than that between patient and doctor. Their relationship is a battle between death and life, with Eliezer on the side of death and Russell as the spokesman for life. Russell prevails, and Eliezer survives. But mere physical life holds little interest for him: "I felt alone, abandoned. Deep inside I discovered a regret: I would have preferred to die."

Kathleen, along with Russell, speaks for life in the novel. Several years earlier, Eliezer had known Kathleen as friend and lover. But they had separated after a year together, largely because Eliezer was still enslaved to his past in the Holocaust. A short time before the accident, Kathleen had turned to Eliezer for help. She herself had had an experience which, while not as destructive as Eliezer's in the Holocaust, brought her to despair. Her marriage had failed, and her attachment to life had almost entirely eroded. She had hoped to find in Eliezer an understanding person whose own past suffering could join him to her in battle against despair. But as the novel opens, Eliezer still feels alienated from life. To him, any alliance with the living is a betrayal of those who died in the Holocaust. How can he embrace life when so many lives were lost? How can he forget the past—as Kathleen hopes he will—when that past seems so much more real and lasting than the fleeting illusions of present existence?

At the beginning of the novel, Eliezer sees that in order to bring Kathleen back from despair he will have to seem to affirm life. He believes that he cannot really change and that he belongs to the dead. But he thinks that he might act "as if" he loves her, that he can pretend to be happy. "I'll have to learn to lie," he

says. He quickly realizes, however, that intimacy with the living, even if it is a masquerade, entails a compromise of his allegiance to the dead. Hence, as we learn near the end of the novel, he steps in front of the taxi, attempting by suicide to escape from the desperate, hopeless situation. Suicide, he apparently thinks, will relieve him from both the horrible pain of remembering the dead and the anxieties of caring for the living.

But the suicide attempt fails, because of the work of Paul Russell, and because, we must think, of the tenacity of life. Even when Eliezer's spirit embraces death, his body wants to live. During his ten weeks' convalescence, he listens to Russell, to Kathleen, to his colleagues from work, and to his friend Gyula, all of whom in some way speak for life. Eliezer, however, cannot forget the dead. As the critic Irving Halperin has observed, "Even if he could, even if he could settle for a 'normal,' satisfying life, sooner or later the past would pursue him with double vengeance, with so much force that he would risk going mad."[5] About his Holocaust experiences, Eliezer says to Kathleen:

I think if I were able to forget I would hate myself. Our stay there planted time bombs within us. From time to time one of them explodes. And then we are nothing but suffering, shame, and guilt. We feel ashamed and guilty to be alive, to eat as much bread as we want, to wear good warm socks in the winter. One of these bombs, Kathleen, will undoubtedly bring about madness. It's inevitable. Anyone who has been there has brought back some of humanity's madness. One day or another, it will come back to the surface.

Eliezer's suffering separates him from the living and gives him, he believes, a superior knowledge of what life is like. There is a degree of arrogance about the tenacity with which Eliezer holds to his own views. He is unwilling or unable to hear and accept

what others say to him. His hurt is too deep, his pain
too complete.

Toward the end of his hospital stay, Eliezer's
resistance weakens slightly. But he cannot embrace
life wholeheartedly; rather, he seeks a halfway
solution. He turns, once again, to lying as a solution.
He says:

I'll learn to lie well and she'll [Kathleen] be happy. It's absurd: lies can give birth to true happiness. Happiness will, as
long as it lasts, seem real. The living like lies, the way they
like to acquire friendships.

With this solution, Eliezer will appear to choose life
and hence will not poison the lives of his associates.
But at the same time he will be true to the dead, who
for him are more important than the living.

Eliezer's commitment to the dead, even his attempt at suicide, evinces an odd kind of concern for
the living. He wishes to protect the living from what
he has seen. He does not wish to poison their attachment to life or to undermine their loves and their
commitments. Therefore he will lie.

Lying, however, is to the question of identity
what suicide is to the question of despair: a false
answer, an inauthentic response. Gyula makes
Eliezer see this. Gyula, an artist, has been Eliezer's
friend for several years. Like Gad in *Dawn*, Gyula
towers above the other characters in the novel. On his
daily visits to the hospital, he paints his friend's portrait. As if to exemplify the process that Wiesel might
wish his own stories to accomplish, this portrait spurs
Eliezer to self-knowledge. As he looks at the finished
portrait, Eliezer sees the face of suffering and despair
which he has been showing to others. He speaks of
the portrait:

I was there, facing me. My whole past was there, facing me.
It was a painting in which black, interspersed with a few red

spots, dominated. The sky was a thick black. The sun, a dark gray. My eyes were a beating red, like Soutine's. They belonged to a man who had seen God commit the most unforgivable crime: to kill without a reason.

Surely this face faithfully expresses Eliezer's experience, yet the interpretation of his self in solely negative terms is a dishonest masquerade that bars him from life's rich diversity. While viewing the portrait, Eliezer again decides to lie to Kathleen and pretend to be happy. Gyula senses what Eliezer has decided. He insists that alleviating the suffering of another person is not a lie but a fulfilment of one's duty to life. "Suffering," he says, "is given to the living, not the dead. . . . It is man's duty to make it cease, not to increase it." To emphasize Eliezer's duty to leave the dead behind, Gyula burns the portrait. With this act he suggests that the mask of suffering must be rejected: it belongs more to the dead than to the living; it tells only a part of the story.

The burning of the portrait also implies that the self is always unfinished and incomplete. However accurate the artist's portrayal of the self—whether by Gyula or by Wiesel himself—aspects of the self always remain undeveloped and unexplored. On this point, Wiesel's view of the self accords with that of the Spanish philosopher Ortega y Gasset:

It is too often forgotten that man is impossible without imagination, without the capacity to invent for himself a concept of life, to "ideate" the character he is going to be. Whether he be original or a plagiarist, man is the novelist of himself. . . . Among . . . possibilities I must choose.[6]

Thus Gyula reminds Eliezer that "man must keep moving, searching, weighing, holding out his hand, offering himself, inventing himself." Eliezer, however, wants to stop moving: he wishes to retain an identity ruled by suffering and despair. Moreover,

it is difficult for him to admit that he would not *necessarily* be lying or pretending in acts of love and friendship. Wiesel's later protagonists can see such acts as creative human possibilities that can be realized in truth and honesty, but this knowledge is hidden from Eliezer.

The ending of *The Accident* leaves the reader uncertain about whether Eliezer will be able to embrace life. It seems as if Eliezer understands the judgment that Gyula has made on him, for he begins to cry. At least he is unsure whether he should continue to see himself only in terms of the Holocaust experience. Near the end of the novel, Eliezer knows he stands at the point of decision:

Everything had been said. The pros and the cons. I would choose the living or the dead. Day or night.

Eliezer must now consider whether there may be a way of embracing the living without betraying the dead. Kathleen's advice to forget the past is too simple for him, but perhaps he may somehow incorporate the past into his existence without the past robbing him of all attachments to present life. Perhaps he can remember the dead in such a way that he will not be unresponsive to the living.

Eliezer's attitude toward the past—and thus his entire being—is placed in question in *The Accident*. In Wiesel's early novels, the self remains open to new possibilities to a small degree, because it maintains a questioning stance. Just as evil and horror intrude abruptly into the lives of his characters, so do goodness, friendship, and love unexpectedly enter: Kathleen and Gyula, for example, unexpectedly offer to care for Eliezer. As a character says in *A Beggar in Jerusalem*, "The mystery of good is no less disturbing than the mystery of evil." The questioner who remains faithful to his own humanity must recognize

and explore the meaning of those moments of goodness. And to such questioning Wiesel turns in his next
novel.

IV

Wiesel turns his interrogatory mind to the questions
of friendship, love, and action in *The Town Beyond the
Wall*, *The Gates of the Forest*, and *A Beggar in
Jerusalem*. There are hints of this change of direction
in the earlier novels, as when Eliezer in *Night*
befriends two young Czechs in the camp at Buna. In
Dawn Elisha records that the love of Gad for a
woman "was an essential part" of Elisha's own life,
for their love reminded him that "there was such a
thing as love and that it brought smiles and joy in its
wake." Elisha also enigmatically muses that perhaps
God was "incarnate in the liking" that he, Elisha,
feels for John Dawson: "The lack of hate between executioner and victim, perhaps this is God." Although
these examples do no more than hint, they indicate
that even in his darkest Holocaust literature Wiesel
attempts to remain alert to the full range of life's experiences. From the beginning, the process of ex-
amining the extreme conditions of life has kept
Wiesel open to the meaning implicit in friendship and
love. But the way to recognition of the secrets of
one's own experience is lengthy. As Yeats said, "It is
so many years before one can believe enough in what
one feels even to know what the feeling is."[7]

The journey leading to a renewal of human relationships takes place in *The Town Beyond the Wall*, a
story of homecoming whose protagonist, Michael,
recapitulates much of the questioning process we
have already observed in Wiesel's works. After the
war, Michael secludes himself in a dingy Paris room

52

Elie Wiesel

where his task is "to create a new skin . . . a new life." Like Eliezer's rejection of Kathleen in *The Accident*, Michael spurns pleas for friendship from Yankel, a fellow survivor. Michael insists that "love is for those who can forget, for those who seek to forget." The senseless death of Yankel awakens in Michael the old anger toward God and the old guilt before the dead. Yankel's death carries him close to madness, while at the same time it reveals to him his inchoate feelings of affection.

The decisive event in Michael's life is his meeting with Pedro, who is a mixture of friend, teacher, and holy man. Pedro arranges Michael's return to his hometown in Hungary, where he is captured and imprisoned by the Communist police. In prison, Michael resists an escape into madness and, surprisingly, turns at the end of the novel to "resume the creation of the world from the void" by retrieving a fellow prisoner from a catatonic silence. Michael's "town beyond the wall" is not the literal town of his birth, for that town has been destroyed and all the Jews there are dead. But beyond the wall of despair and death and the past lies a town, waiting to be created, of hope and life and the future. And the place to begin the creative act exists in the immediate situation, which in Michael's case involves the one fellow prisoner. Life, Michael learns, must be directed to the living.

In *The Town Beyond the Wall* Wiesel makes interrogation the central structural component of the narrative, for the entire story is related during Michael's interrogation by the police. Their interrogation is ironically called "prayer," since the prisoner, like a praying Jew, must stand until he confesses or goes mad. The "prayers" in this book are no longer inquiries directed to God, but instead are questions directed to Michael. The police want to know who

helped him enter the country. Other questions arise from within Michael: can he remain faithful to his friend and refuse to reveal who assisted him? Can he suffer the agony of this "prayer" to save a friend? Indeed, Michael the interrogator is being interrogated: his fidelity in friendship is on trial.

Michael, in a tendency increasingly prominent in Wiesel's vision, translates the man/man relationship into an enactment of the God/man relationship. The Hasids believe that God hides in the least likely stranger, ready to surprise the unsuspecting. Wiesel's attribution of religious intensity to friendship reflects this notion. Michael—the name means "Who is like God?"—discovers the divine presence in those persons close to him. Hence he refuses to betray his friend, and he assists his fellow prisoner. Pedro's remembered words inspire Michael: "He who thinks about God, forgetting man, runs the risk of mistaking his goal: God may be your next-door neighbor."

In considering the meaning of friendship, Wiesel discloses the assumption fundamental to the process of questioning. Michael remarks: "But to say, 'What is God? What is the world? What is my friend?' is to say that I have someone to talk to, someone to ask a direction of." The drama of interrogation leads to a recognition of the significance of relationships in the lives of Wiesel's characters; at the same time, it reveals that a relationship is the necessary foundation for interrogation. The possibility of asking a question is founded on the notion that we are not, as Eliezer assumes in *Night*, completely "alone in the world." Furthermore, meaningful human existence is involved less with building relationships than with questioning the meaning of those relationships that one already has established.

The element of questioning carries a still further

significance in *The Town Beyond the Wall*, since a question—why does Michael wish to return to his hometown?—provides the chief element of narrative suspense. This question, which Pedro asks continually and which Michael cannot answer, is resolved when Michael confronts a man who looked on passively while the Jews were being deported. Michael realizes that

This was the thing I had wanted to understand ever since the war. Nothing else. How a human being can remain indifferent. The executioners I understood; also the victims, though with more difficulty. For the others, all the others, those who were neither for nor against, those who sprawled in passive patience . . . those who were permanently and merely spectators—all those were closed to me, incomprehensible.

In one of the most dramatic moments in Wiesel's work, Michael indicts a character who has acted as a mere spectator "with the sin—no, the punishment—of indifference."[8] That indictment brings into question the model of self-interpretation that we observed in *The Accident*, in which a person plays an invented role and in which there is a split between the self and its role, and a split between being and acting. To play at living, Michael suggests, is insufficient: merely to pretend happiness, friendship, and love leads to an indifference in which the real action and death of men are viewed as morally neutral. Michael says to the spectator, "People like you retreat to an ivory tower and say to themselves, 'All the world's a stage and all the men and women merely players.'" In Michael's view, the Holocaust is a repudiation of the ethical nihilism that he sees as the real meaning of the idea of life as a game:

If living in peace means evolving in nothingness, you accept the nothingness. The Jews in the courtyard of the

synagogue? Nothing. The shrieks of women gone mad in cattle cars? Nothing. The silence of thirsty children? Nothing. All that's a game, you tell yourself. A movie! Fiction: seen and forgotten. I tell you, you're a machine for the fabrication of nothingness.

In contrast to the view that life is a game and the self a player, Michael affirms what Pedro calls "simplicity," a state in which there is neither disguise nor pretense:

"I believe in simplicity," Pedro said. "When one loves, one must say: I love you. When one wants to weep, one must say: I want to weep. When one becomes aware that existence is too heavy a burden, one must say: I want to die. . . . In driving Adam out of Paradise . . . God merely deprived him of the power of simplicity."

For Michael a return to simplicity means admitting into his life things as ordinary as working, loving, being a friend, and having a family. In thus redeeming his own life, Michael begins to recover that "condition of complete simplicity," the simplicity "costing not less than everything."[9]

But we misunderstand the complexity of Wiesel's interrogation of the self if we think that his world divides neatly into victims, executioners, and spectators and that in it are persons who simply play at living and others who embody the life of simplicity. As the representatives of these different life possibilities confront one another, Wiesel suggests that the self is multidimensional. Michael seizes this insight: "Down deep, I thought, man is not only an executioner, not only a victim, not only a spectator: he is all three at once." The problem is not that of either being a person who invents himself or being a person who simply is what he is, but rather that of being both persons at the same time. People are simultaneously authentic and inauthentic. Not only is the self a

quester, without identity or home or firm mooring; the self, speaking out of ancient wisdom, is also teacher and guide, possessing, like Gyula and Pedro, quiet confidence and great simplicity.

Michael's movement toward simplicity does not end in the stasis of a completed self, for other questions are left to explore. Questions about God and evil and suffering remain unanswered, because they are unanswerable. Michael's self-progression, however, does bring the equilibrium that accompanies the capacity to feel compassion toward another person. By caring, he comes home to the only place he can be—where he is—and there, even in a prison cell, he can act to alleviate suffering. Michael's prayer, "God of my childhood, show me the way that leads to myself," finds a response, and the way "leads to another human being." In moving toward another human being, he finds a place in which the hidden simplicity of life and the questions of man join in dialogue. There, he must dare "to ask the great questions and ask them again, to look up at another, a friend, and to look up again: if two questions stand face to face, that's at least something. It's at least a victory." As Gyula says in *The Accident*: "Maybe God is dead, but man is alive. The proof: he is capable of friendship."

The town to which Michael returns is unlike the town from which he was torn by the Holocaust. Yet it is surprisingly like that town, for it is a place where persons care for one another and where they share their hopes and their despair, their pasts and their futures.

V

Much of what we have seen of the lives of Wiesel's

protagonists involves a determined withdrawal from action. Returning from the Holocaust denuded of self and stripped of a community in which to act, Wiesel's central characters have little capacity for or interest in action. Indeed, Wiesel's early protagonists are almost incapable of initiating action. They are carried along by guilt and anger and despair; their lives are characterized by what happens to them rather than by what they make happen. Eliezer of *Night* is the passive victim of the Holocaust; Elisha in *Dawn* acts only at the command of another person; in *The Accident* Eliezer attempts through death to escape the possibility of action. Similarly, the early lives of Michael in *The Town Beyond the Wall* and Gregor in *The Gates of the Forest* drift without a firm rooting in concrete action.

This inability to interact meaningfully with the external world reinforces the reader's impression that the primary focus of Wiesel's work is on character, not on plot or action. Indeed, Wiesel at times accentuates the interest in character by telling the reader the outcome of the action at the beginning of the narrative: for example, we learn in the Prologue of *Dawn* that Elisha will kill John Dawson. Moreover, Wiesel's plotting, especially in the longer narratives, is often loose, providing only a frame for the exploration of the inner lives of his characters.

Despite the protagonists' retreat from action and the emphasis on the characters' interior life, the drama of interrogation is a preparation for action. The preparation occurs in several stages: first, the protagonist secludes himself for a period of introspection, then a compelling individual intrudes and attempts to engage the protagonist with the living, then narrative interest focuses on the contrast between the protagonist's inaction and his friend's willingness to love and act, and finally, the protagonist,

after enduring the loss of the friend and after further suffering, arrives at the moment of choice and action. *The Town Beyond the Wall, The Gates of the Forest,* and *A Beggar in Jerusalem* all reflect this pattern.

Wiesel's protagonists move toward action because they wish to regain a story for their own lives. They realize that without action there is no story to life: without action, one's life is only an evocative background with no center of concern. David, the protagonist of *A Beggar in Jerusalem*, suggests as much when he remarks, "I'm also looking for a story." His search for a story takes him to fight and, he hopes, to die in the 1967 Arab-Israeli War. He hopes for some definitive action that will give shape to an amorphous, storyless existence. His plan involves an agreement with an Israeli soldier named Katriel that if one of them dies in the war, the survivor will tell the other's story. But it is Katriel who is missing in action: hence David faces the problem of whether in addition to telling Katriel's story he should live out that story. At the end of the narrative, David takes Katriel's place and marries his widow. With this action, David, like the rest of Wiesel's later protagonists, builds a story for his own existence.

In sharp contrast to these protagonists' inability to act is the capacity of their close companions to commit themselves. The secret of Katriel's power and of the power of Gyula, Gad, and Pedro is that, although they too have suffered and have been close to madness, they are still able to engage life through self-initiated action. In the Arab-Israeli War, Katriel is missing in action. It is toward willingness to lose oneself in action that Wiesel's protagonists must move. Only in this way will they be able to tell the stories of the dead and create stories for their own lives.

In Wiesel's perspective, the resolve to act is the

culmination of an ongoing process of self-interrogation, self-creation, and self-discovery. Michael in *The Town Beyond the Wall*, Gregor in *The Gates of the Forest*, and David in *A Beggar in Jerusalem* come decisively to the moment of action. They apparently realize that "sooner or later . . . one has to take sides—if one is to remain human."[10]

The Hasidic rebbe who assumes such a powerful role in the final pages of *The Gates of the Forest* brings Gregor to see the necessity of choosing. To Gregor's question of how belief in God is possible after the Holocaust, the rebbe replies, "How can you *not* believe in God after what has happened?" But as the rebbe's wisdom enables him to see, belief or nonbelief is not a final answer. He says to Gregor: "I ask you a question and dare you answer: 'What is there left for us to do?'" With a despair greater than the antinomy of hope and despair that tears at Gregor and a faith that transcends the opposition of belief and unbelief, the rebbe continues to probe the question of doing. There are no adequate answers, either theological or philosophical or psychoanalytical, yet the individual must continue to face life, and to do what he can to alleviate suffering, to respond to the need of persons to be loved, and to act in behalf of friendship. David states the dilemma: "Do you understand now that love, no matter how personal or universal, is not a solution? And that outside of love there is no solution?" Having only proximate answers to unanswerable questions, Wiesel's protagonists must nonetheless take courage and act.

His emphasis on action suggests that Wiesel's questioning is not a sophistry that engages argumentation for its own sake nor a cynical detachment from the concrete problems of life. Wiesel's interrogation is a process in which a person recovers a reserve of integrity, wholeness, and health. The self arrives at the

state Ortega y Gasset calls *ensimismarse*, "within-one-selfness," which means so taking a stand within the self as to empower oneself to act freely in the relationships in which one stands.[11] Interrogation, while it involves solitary self-exploration, does not allow Wiesel's protagonists to withdraw from their external situations; rather, it links them more closely to that situation. The end of the process, Wiesel suggests, is not self-enclosed thinking or solitary contemplation: it is action on behalf of that which is disclosed by the process of interrogation. What confronts us in Wiesel's work is a continuing process involving both enaction of those insights that are disclosed through questioning and questioning of those insights that inform action.

In seeing the importance of both insight and action for Wiesel, we do well to remember that most of his protagonists, like the author himself, carry the imprint of two distinct influences, one received from the mother and the other from the father. These two influences are reflected in the tension between mysticism and action, between esoteric wisdom and the practical spirit of Jewish humanism. These two dimensions do battle in Wiesel's work, and both are integral to the full image of the self that he portrays. In his work, the impulse to turn toward mystical solitude is checked by a historical awareness of the desperate needs of human beings. Similarly, the loss of the self in frenetic activism is prevented by listening to the dark mysteries buried in the self.

Action comes to occupy a large place in Wiesel's sensibility because in the Holocaust he experienced so catastrophically the consequences of the failure to act. In Wiesel's view, it was indifference on the part of executioners and spectators that brought about the destruction of the six million. And storytelling is Wiesel's action against indifference and in support of

friendship. "We tell the tale of the Holocaust," he says, "to save the world from indifference."

But if Wiesel's stories are to awaken the reader from indifference, they must initiate him into the drama of interrogation. The reader is encouraged to enter into the process that Wiesel's narratives portray. As we have seen, that process includes inquiring into the self, attending to significant relationships, envisioning and effecting meaningful action. The drama of interrogation is a process by which one comes to have a life and a story of one's own.

4

....

A New Beginning

In Elie Wiesel's work the Holocaust is an ending. Even in the death camps he knew that the experience marked "the end of an era, the end of a world." Yet a question seems always to accompany this conviction: "Are we still capable of beginning all over again?"

Over the years in numerous books, Wiesel has endeavored to respond to this question affirmatively. The feeling of ending, however, burdens his early protagonists, and their efforts to begin again are largely abortive. In *The Town Beyond the Wall*, *The Gates of the Forest*, *A Beggar in Jerusalem*, and *The Oath*, the dynamic necessity of beginning again gathers power and establishes itself against the forces of ending. From these works, there hesitantly yet steadily arises this daring affirmation: "When He created man, God gave him a secret—and that secret was not how to begin but how to begin again."

This affirmation is related to an important dimension in Wiesel's understanding of the Jewish conception of man. In creating the world, the God of Israel did not entirely destroy formlessness and darkness, but He made man in His image to continue the fight against them. Wiesel makes this point clearly: "We cannot create; we are too weak to create. But we can re-create: we can complete; we can achieve what he [God] began." For Wiesel, the strug-

63

gle against formlessness and darkness goes on every day in the actions people choose and in the words they speak.

One of the most dramatic examples of a new beginning in Wiesel's literature occurs at the end of *The Town Beyond the Wall*. Michael is in his prison cell, alone with a young boy who is in a catatonic stupor. This Silent One, as he is called, is at the end of his struggle—he neither speaks nor acts. Michael himself is engaged in a struggle against madness. At this moment of crisis, Michael hears within himself the voice of his friend Pedro, who says to him: "Re-create the universe. Restore that boy's sanity. Cure him. He'll save you." And then the narrator reports:

Michael welcomed the dawn as a new man. His strength flowed back. He was suddenly responsible for a life that was an inseparable part of the life of mankind. He would fight. He would resume the creation of the world from the void.

The last pages of the novel recount the way in which Michael re-creates a world by reaching out to the young boy. Michael battles against chaos, silence, darkness; his weapon is language. And finally, after a terrible struggle, the boy responds to Michael. And as Pedro promised, the act of curing the boy saves Michael, for by taking responsibility for the boy—by responding to him—Michael discovers a world for himself.

We see here a pattern that occurs throughout Wiesel's narratives. First, two persons meet, one of whom has reached an ending. The other calls to him, and through the power of language a new beginning occurs. Wiesel tells this story again and again: how the possibility of the re-creation of a world exists in an encounter between human beings.

The Gates of the Forest, Wiesel's most complex narrative, powerfully displays the way in which peo-

ple can begin again. The novel has four distinct parts, "Spring," "Summer," "Autumn," and "Winter." The seasonal motif signals Wiesel's concern for the re-creation of a world, since nature's yearly cycle represents continual rebirth. But the motif functions somewhat ironically, for the novel suggests a difference between the re-creation that occurs in nature and that which occurs in the historical life of a human being. The renewal of nature each year is automatic, and it follows a predictable pattern of growth and development. The re-creation of a human life is more uncertain and even more mysterious than the cycle of the seasons. It reflects less the predictable process of natural growth than it does the interaction of unexpected events and encounters. The re-creation of a life depends on the honesty of a person's questioning, the power of his memory, and the scope of his imagination. These three processes— questioning, remembering, imagining—work together in the re-creation of a human life in the work of Elie Wiesel.

But why does Wiesel speak of "re-creation" instead of "creation" when he speaks of beginning again? *The Gates of the Forest* is re-creation because, like all Wiesel's stories, it exists in the near and distant past. In the near past, we see a victim and a survivor enduring and going beyond the Holocaust. In the distant past, we see how the protagonist relives a story much older than his own. The incidents in his life correspond to and resonate with incidents in the collective story of Jewish experience from ancient times to the present. We have already seen these two levels coexisting in *Night*, in which Eliezer's journey corresponds to and reverses aspects of the Biblical story of the Exodus.

Wiesel's work is a re-creation, then, because he combines material from his own and the larger

Jewish past. The re-creative work of the storyteller differs from the creative work of God: God, in making the world, was creating, because there was no past with which to work. The storyteller's work resembles God's—and is thereby in Wiesel's view a "sacred" work—but does not equal it.

The Gates of the Forest recapitulates (often by reversing) elements of the Jewish tradition. We can, for example, understand the four parts of the novel in relationship to four motifs from Jewish history. The first part, "Spring," echoes the experience of chaos and creation in Genesis; "Summer" corresponds especially to the experience of anti-Semitism in the Christian West; "Autumn" recalls the action of the Jewish rebels through the centuries; "Winter" emphasizes religious community and family solidarity as responses to loneliness in human life. To view the novel in this way does not suggest that Wiesel consciously organized his story with these motifs in mind. Indeed, he seems to compose by a process of association rather than by following a tight organizational scheme. This view, however, emphasizes how the novel, like all Wiesel's narratives, reaches beyond itself into the long history of Jewish experience. By attending to some aspects of the Jewishness of Wiesel's novel, we can better see how he transmutes this distinctive tradition into a resource that speaks to the self-understanding of all persons.

I

In the Biblical story of creation, God began when the earth was "unformed and void, and darkness was upon the face of the deep." The story continues: "And God said: 'Let there be light.' And there was light" (Genesis 1:2-3). In Wiesel's novel there are

echoes and reversals of this primordial scene. In the Holocaust there is the reversal. It is as if someone had stepped out into the cosmos and said: "Let there be night. Let all the things that have been won in the struggle against formlessness and darkness slip back into chaos."

The opening of *The Gates of the Forest* reflects this reversal. The protagonist has escaped from the Nazis and is hiding in a forest not far from his hometown in Hungary. He has rejected his Jewish name, "Gavriel," and now calls himself "Gregor." Gavriel means "man of God," or, "God has shown Himself mighty," and in Judaism the name often belongs to a person who brings a special message from God.[1] In the days of the Holocaust, this name is no longer appropriate, for Wiesel's protagonist has no message from God and God has not overcome his enemies.

The name "Gregor" is significant as well, for its Greek root means "he who is awake," or "he who is watching." In many ways, the entire novel portrays the process of Gregor's awakening. The motif is established in the first scene of the novel with several references to Gregor's awakening. The forest, moreover, symbolizes one dimension of the reality to which he awakens. In the forest, Gregor knows "a sense of security"; he feels "close to the earth" and feels a primeval unity with nature, much as Adam did in the Garden of Eden. Gregor has a renewed sense of a "harmony" that "may not be destroyed," for the forest is "before creation." He feels aligned with the "ancient and secret design," and secluded from the ravages of history being played out in the town below.

But the forest has another side as well. While it provides solace, it frightens as well. Gregor has "learned that the true forest is the one that drives

wolves mad and makes men thirst for blood and compassion. There was no use running away from this
forest, it is everywhere. . . ." The forest is terrifying,
in part, because it is the realm of freedom and
possibility. By hiding in the forest, Gregor removes
himself from the forces of enslavement and death
that are destroying the Jewish community. He has
been forced out of his ordered pre-Holocaust world
into a realm of freedom and choice.

Gregor can remain in the solitude of the forest
apart from his fellow man or he can leave the forest
and join the common struggles. Before he can choose,
however, a nameless stranger invades his hiding
place. The stranger's first response to Gregor is
laughter:

Then for the first time he heard the laughter. Gregor shud-
dered and his legs became weak. Behind every tree and
within every shred of cloud someone was laughing.

This laughter belongs to a person who has been
driven to the brink of madness by the events in the
town below. As the trees and clouds themselves take
up the laughter, it severs the harmony between
Gregor and nature.

This opening scene reflects the way in which the
horror of historical events leads Gregor and other
Wiesel protagonists to consider but finally reject a
retreat into the solitude and comfort of nature.
Wiesel's character dwells at the gates of the forest,
not in the forest. To dwell in the forest would be to
escape from history: it would be to live apart from the
struggles of one's fellows in the town. To dwell at the
gates of the forest means to look in two directions:
toward the experience of primordial unity with the
natural world, and toward the responsibility to join
with other persons in re-creating a world.

But how is such re-creation to take place? The

Biblical story of creation provides the pattern: God responded to chaos with language. The nameless stranger introduces the pattern when he says to Gregor, "Names played an important part in creation, didn't they? It was by naming things that God made them." Gregor himself takes the first step in re-creation when he bestows the name "Gavriel" on the stranger. True to his new name, Gavriel gives a message about God. But instead of reporting God's efforts for the people of Israel, he relates the failure and absence of God. Instead of describing how God's people are flourishing, he informs Gregor that the Jews are being systematically exterminated.

Gavriel's message reverses yet another element of the Biblical creation story. In the Bible, a principal theme is that of beginning. Genesis—the word means "beginning"—highlights the first man and woman, the first sin, the first murder. It tells about the beginnings of the people of Israel with Abraham and with the Exodus. But Gavriel's story emphasizes ending. His story, Gregor realizes, comes "from another time, another world," because it is founded on ending, rather than on beginning. Wiesel states the first line of his new creation story, "In the beginning there was the Holocaust. We must therefore start all over again."[2]

Gavriel, however, does not stop with the story of destruction. Gregor, he says, must join in the battle against chaos; the two of them together can locate meaning on which to build a new world. Alone they will go mad, but together they can make a new beginning:

When I came last night to this town I had no idea that I would meet you. If our paths have crossed, it must be that our meeting conceals some meaning. Let's discover it and study it. If we find nothing, and our meeting seems to have no significance, then we must impose one upon it.

The old world seems to have ended. The first step in re-creating a world is to tell the story of that ending. The second step is to question the significance of the meeting of two persons.

The meeting of Gregor and Gavriel in the forest reverberates with the two kinds of past times mentioned earlier. First, in the near past, two persons meet and determine to live their lives in relationship to each other. This level, however, recalls the story from the distant past of God's meeting the people of Israel. Gavriel corresponds to God in the Biblical story. There God, who refuses to name Himself, is the mysterious one who both hides and shows Himself; He makes a promise, which becomes the basis for relationships and the reason for the Israelites' existence. Gavriel does the same in Wiesel's story. Just as the ancient Israelite centered his life on the God of the covenant, so Gregor vows to live in order to love and understand Gavriel: "This will be the aim of my existence. I'll become him in order to understand him better, to understand and love him, or to love him without understanding."

The promise of a new beginning in friendship is aborted, however, when Gavriel, to save his friend, surrenders to the Hungarian police at the close of the first part of the novel. With the promise of a new world thwarted, Gregor must again start over, carrying with him the memory of his meeting with Gavriel in the forest.

II

Wiesel has commented that, as a young boy in Sighet, he had very little understanding of or interest in Christianity. In *The Gates of the Forest* he questions Christianity, its history and the way in which it has in-

teracted with and affected his individual past and the collective past of all Jews. He aims not so much to accuse Christians as to understand them.

The novel's action moves in "Summer" to the Christian world when Gregor leaves the forest to seek refuge in the town close by. Apparently the Jew, if he is to survive, must attempt to ally himself with the non-Jewish world. Gregor seeks refuge with a simple peasant woman named Maria, who was a servant in his home before the war. The Christian world as a whole has as yet given the Jew only indifference and death. But an individual Christian, Wiesel suggests, may be compassionate; thus Gregor goes to Maria.

Gregor's refuge with Maria marks another new beginning in the novel. Again, the initial step is for someone to tell what is happening to the Jews. Gavriel's message now becomes Gregor's message. Although she is a simple woman, Maria understands Gregor's story, and she devises a plan to save him, just as Gavriel did. She understands that to survive "Gregor must have an identity, a home, a past, a story." She fashions a story—she builds an imaginative world—that can shelter Gregor from the chaos that threatens him.

Maria's strategy is ingenious: Gregor is to pretend to be the deaf-mute son of Maria's disreputable sister, Ileana. Thinking that Gregor cannot hear what they are saying, the villagers confess to him the deepest secrets of their lives, dwelling particularly on their relationships with his lascivious "mother." The disguise works well until Gregor is cast as Judas in a school play designed to portray the Christians' "hatred of the Jews and its justification." During the performance, he reveals himself as a Jew and the villagers in the audience attack Gregor as though he were really Judas, "the murderer of God." He is saved only by the intervention of Petruskanu, the

mayor, who delivers him to the Jewish partisans in the forest nearby.

Wiesel uses this incident to point out several elements in his understanding of the relationship between Jews and Christians. First, Maria and Petruskanu's goodness reminds us that some Christians acted courageously to save Jews during the Holocaust. Indeed, Maria and Petruskanu, like Gavriel, are compared with the divine. Gregor sees his protector as "the divine old Maria," and of Petruskanu the villagers speak "fearfully, with lowered voices, as if he were in league with some celestial or diabolical power." He, "like a God, would never allow himself to be seen by his subjects." Gavriel, Petruskanu, and Maria are associated with God largely because they are willing to take responsibility for Gregor. Wiesel suggests that, insofar as God is present in Gregor's world, He is present in the concrete acts that one human being does for another. The godlike action of these characters, we should note, contrasts ironically with Wiesel's portrayal of the God of Israel, who did not intervene to save His people.

While Wiesel remembers the few Christians who helped the Jews, he does not soften his charges against Christians. In the novel itself, the question is this: how could the villagers on one day protect and even love Gregor, and on the next attempt to kill him? How do simple Christians come to be metamorphosed into diabolical, bloodthirsty monsters?

The numerous references to the theater in the novel are important to the response to these questions. For example, after Gavriel's capture in "Spring," the narrator comments: "Intermission was over. The play began again." The play here, of course, is one in which the Nazis are executioners and Jews are victims; Gregor escaped from this drama for a few days in the forest. In the town, Gregor volun-

tarily takes the role devised by Maria as a protection from the other, dangerous role the Nazis have imposed on him. Similarly, the villagers play roles that do not coincide with their thoughts and feelings, for underneath the tranquil surface of their lives, there rage the torrents of energy, chiefly sexual in nature, that they confess to Gregor. Their roles as simple, God-fearing peasants cover dark and violent passions.

In the midst of all this role playing, the school drama becomes a crucial incident. The situation is multilayered. "Gregor" is actually "Gavriel," a Jew hiding from the Nazis. He pretends to be Maria's deaf-mute nephew. The villagers impose upon him the role of confessor. He assumes the stage role of Judas, the betrayer of Jesus. With the play, Wiesel exposes an important element in Christian anti-Semitism: the role of Judas from the Christian story has been imposed on all Jews, who have thus been branded as betrayers deserving of death. Some Christians have rationalized the killing of Jews by making Judas and, by extension, all Jews responsible for Jesus's death.

Christians as well as Jews are victimized by one-dimensional thinking. We see this in the way in which the villagers are easily duped during the performance of the school play. They are easily deluded because, as the village priest admits, they are living "in ignorance and among lies, content with easy explanations." The ritual of the play works by means of simplification. First, the audience simplifies Gregor-Judas into Judas, the actual murderer of God. The lines of demarcation are sharply drawn:

Then, all of a sudden, the whole thing came alive, became clear. On one side the villain, on the other, the virtuous, the righteous. Here was a language they could understand. Everything had become perfectly simple.

The villagers are duped again when Gregor exalts Judas as a saint. They repudiate their entire tradition

by declaring that Judas "is innocent and we humbly implore his forgiveness." Gregor destroys this simplification as well, declaring, "I am a Jew and my name is a Jewish name, Gavriel," and the crowd again becomes a mob and moves to execute him.

The basis of this scene is Wiesel's insistence on the power of language and storytelling. For him, language can be creative, even redemptive; the worlds that persons create with language can be a haven from disorder. Gregor is saved by the story that Maria devises. Yet human beings can also be victimized by the stories they create. Such victimization occurred in the Holocaust when the complexity of millions of human stories was robbed by Nazi propaganda. The Holocaust itself, Wiesel has said, was a "huge simplification." He shows that language can oversimplify, can reduce, and when it does, people can make excuses for the release of the darkest passions of the human soul. Language, as Gregor comes to see, is two-sided: "The human voice brings people together and separates them. Brick by brick, stone by stone the voice builds walls. . . . Eventually the voice becomes a prison."

Is there any release from the prisons of language that human beings create for themselves? Can one avoid being duped by one's own stories? Wiesel has no easy answer to these questions, but he points to several safeguards. First, a spirit of questioning such as that his literature embodies guards against living "in ignorance and among lies, content with easy explanations." Persistent questioning provides a buffer, albeit a fragile one, against the tendency to simplify and thereby reduce human beings. Second, Wiesel would judge any story against this criterion: does it serve to protect and enrich life, or does it serve to justify indiscriminate cruelty?

Analysis of Wiesel's third response to these

issues requires a closer examination of the symbolism of the forest. At the end of the novel, Gregor speaks of the two possibilities for his life: living inside and living outside the forest. Inside the forest "simplicity is possible. . . . And unity, too." Gregor wishes to be free of roles that trap and delude him; he wishes to live so that "there is no divorce between the self and its image, between being and acting." In the forest, Gregor would not have to disguise himself as a deaf-mute son of a Christian whore in order to survive. A few persons, such as Gavriel, seem to be able to eschew role playing and achieve a unity of the self. But such an ideal is unattainable for most persons, and it may not be altogether praiseworthy, because it often requires isolation and rejection of human relationships.

But if life inside the forest is an almost unattainable goal, life outside the forest appears undesirable. "Outside, things are too complicated; too many roads are open, too many voices call and your own is so easily lost. The self crumbles." This crumbling or scattering of the self is what happens to the villagers during the performance of the play: as they follow first one story, then another, they lose themselves.

What then does Wiesel propose as a solution to this dilemma? He suggests a rhythm of the self that moves between the simplicity of the forest and the complication of the town. In the town we inevitably assume roles that do not display the self accurately. One either assumes conflicting roles simultaneously—in which case the self is divided against itself—or reduces oneself and others to a simplistic role—in which case we risk deluding the self or brutalizing the other. To counter these tendencies, Wiesel suggests we need to return to the forest periodically. At least in imagination, we must allow the world we inhabit to

drop away; we must experience the primordial harmony that the forest symbolizes.

One element of Wiesel's rendering of Christian
anti-Semitism remains to be explicated: that of Jesus.
There is a large number of correspondences between
Wiesel's protagonists and Jesus. *The Gates of the
Forest* opens with a scene that echoes the crucifixion
story. Like Christ after his burial, Gregor is in a cave
whose opening is covered with a stone. Gregor is later
cared for by Maria and pretends to be the son of an
unmarried woman, and the villagers see him as "innocent" and "free of sin." During the play, there are
several parallels between the experience of Gregor-
Judas and Jesus' crucifixion: a thief escapes while
Gregor is being reviled, the crowd is ready "to add
another cross to those of Golgotha." Later in the
novel, Gregor, like Jesus, invokes the words of the
Psalmist and cries, "God, my God, why have you for-
saken me?"

One might explain these correspondences by
pointing to the fact that both the New Testament
writers and Wiesel drew imagery from the Hebrew
Bible. This explanation is partially adequate, but it
overlooks the deliberate point that Wiesel is making
about Christians and Jews. "I believe," he has said,
"that the Christians betrayed the Christ more than
the Jews did." Jews, not Christians, have more
nearly followed in the path of Jesus as patient suf-
ferers. Jews were reviled and hated and finally
crucified by collective madness in the Holocaust.
Christians, on the other hand, have more closely
followed in the path of Judas as betrayers of Jesus'
teaching.

Part of Wiesel's response to this perverse history
of anti-Semitism is anger, although sadness is more
strongly evoked. When Maria prays to Jesus, Gregor
entreats her to "let him be. He, too, has been changed

into a cloud." Wiesel also let Jesus be, for he knows that the followers of Jesus, not Jesus himself, are responsible for the madness of Christian anti-Semitism. This is made clear in *A Beggar in Jerusalem* when a character imagines a conversation with Jesus on the day of his crucifixion. After Jesus hears what his followers will later do in his name, he says, "I want my heritage to be a gift of compassion and hope, not a punishment in blood!" Wiesel's voice sounds through in the words of his narrator: "His sobs broke my heart and I sought to comfort him."

The history of the relations between Christians and Jews has included much death and violence. In recalling it, Wiesel attempts to understand the old world that has been destroyed and to move toward beginning a new world in which understanding will guard against the repetition of the old evil.

III

In "Autumn" the scene shifts back to the forest where Gregor joins a small band of Jewish partisans who are involved in underground activity against the Nazis. Now the forest is the scene of activity, not of passivity and seclusion. In one of those strange coincidences that occur throughout Wiesel's work, Gregor is reunited with Leib, a young man whom he had known years earlier. Gregor delivers to Leib and his comrades the terrible message that Gavriel had related to him. On hearing of the destruction of all the Jews, Leib suggests that perhaps "the human race has reached the end of the road."

Leib is another bold, active character, like Gavriel and Maria. He recognizes that the life the characters have known has ended and starts immediately to fashion a new beginning. He devises a

plan: Clara (Leib's lover) and Gregor will go into the town to secure information about Gavriel, who they think may still be held captive by the local police. Again role playing is important, for in Leib's plan, Clara pretends to be the lover of Gregor during the three days they are in the town. The plan fails miserably: Gavriel is not found, and Leib is captured by the police.

Leib's action, even though it fails, contrasts with the passive suffering and victimization sometimes portrayed by Wiesel. With Leib and the partisans Wiesel shows the possibility of rebellion and resistance.

What enables a person to reject the role of victim and to rebel against his persecutors? To answer this question, Wiesel evokes the story of Jesus, who is often portrayed as the embodiment of passive acceptance. He went to his death accepting his crucifixion as the will of God. How, Wiesel asks, could Jesus have avoided such a death? And could the Jews have avoided submitting to death in the Holocaust as though it were the will of God?

Gregor provides a response when he says to Maria: "Did you know that Christ was a Jew? . . . Do you know why he was crucified? I'll tell you: because he never learned to laugh." Laughter would have been a gesture of defiance of the executioners. The laughter would have signalled a rejection of the idea of passive suffering being redemptive and praiseworthy. This laughter would signify defiance of a God who asks for the death of his followers as a mark of their fidelity. Wiesel suggests that undeserved suffering, passively accepted and actively praised, must be unequivocally rejected.

All of this relates to what we saw earlier about the way in which Jews have followed the path of Jesus. The portrayal of Jesus in the New Testament

draws heavily on the image of the Suffering Servant in the Hebrew Bible, especially Isaiah, chapter 53. Judaism and Christianity share this traditional imagery, but Jewishness involves other elements as well. Wiesel believes that Jews should affirm life and act to preserve it. They should not glorify death and undeserved suffering as the means by which life and redemption are served.

Rebellion means refusing to interpret oneself as a victim of forces of evil and destruction. Rebellion also means action in behalf of friendship and love. One rebels against evil in order to make room for friendship. Gavriel, Maria, Petruskanu, Leib—all undertake such action in *The Gates of the Forest*. And finally, at Leib's instigation, Gregor too rebels by risking his life in an effort to rescue Gavriel from prison.

This action creates conflicts among several elements of the new world that Gregor is attempting to create. First, there is conflict between Gregor's friendship for Gavriel and for Leib. At one point during his mission in the town, Gregor risks exposing Leib to danger: "Gregor felt torn between Leib and Gavriel. . . . To choose one of them meant to betray the other." And he is in a conflict between his friendship for Leib and his own love for Clara. His mission requires that he pretend to love Clara, but finally he must confess, "I'm no longer acting." To maintain his friendship with Leib, Gregor must deny his affection for Clara; to disclose his love would be to betray his friend.

The new world that Gregor finds among the partisans quickly becomes tragic, for he faces contradictory claims upon his fidelity. And in addition to such unresolvable conflicts, the new world, like the old, must come to an end. Leib is captured, and Gregor is once again "at end of an epoch, of a friendship." But

this ending is two-sided: Gregor loses Leib but gains the possibility of loving Clara.

The conflicts that Gregor experiences in his relationships give rise to a sense of guilt. This becomes explicit when Gregor returns from the town to report to the partisans what has happened to Leib. The partisans place Gregor on trial, interrogating him about the events that led to Leib's capture. Gregor relates his story five times. The first four times he reports accurately and somewhat dispassionately. As he begins to relate the story for a fifth time, however, Gregor confesses:

I take all responsibility. But it wasn't an accident. It was a betrayal. It's too easy to blame chance. You want someone guilty: here I am.

Gregor is lying, as Clara soon informs the partisans. But there is some truth in the lie, a truth Gregor learns about himself. He reflects on his insight: "Look: I have ordered the *Yetzer Hara*, the spirit of evil, to come out of myself and be seen. All of its unspeakable desires, I make mine; I acknowledge in myself the most disgusting acts and ambitions. . . ." The truth that Gregor "would never deny" is that, in some unexplained way, he betrayed his friend Leib.

Gregor's confession is difficult to understand and accept. Like the partisans, the reader wishes to exonerate Gregor and to assure him that he is suffering under an exaggerated sense of responsibility—that he is confusing the workings of an overly scrupulous conscience with real guilt. This simple and plausible explanation is, however, a misinterpretation of Wiesel's perspective on guilt and responsibility. Gregor judges himself guilty because he is alive and free while his friends Gavriel and Leib have been arrested and presumably killed. Perhaps Gregor finds himself guilty because he realizes that in certain cir-

cumstances he might allow the death of others in order to remain alive himself; that he too would act out of self-interest to survive; that to have Clara he would allow and will the death of his friend Leib. "Is there anywhere," Wiesel asks in another place, "a love untainted by betrayal?" Gregor seems to think not. Hence he feels himself to be guilty.

We might think that by acknowledging and accepting this kind of guilt Gregor burdens his life with a morbid sense of self-indictment. Actually his confession leads to inner freedom and joy. After the confession, "he knew that he would survive, alive, but conquered." What is conquered is the illusion that in any new world that he might create he can escape tragedy and guilt. Life in the town inevitably involves conflicting imperatives. For Gregor to live, Gavriel must die; for Gregor truly to love Clara, Leib must die. Such conflicts, Wiesel suggests, are unavoidable. Only through acknowledging them and taking upon oneself the guilt that attaches to any decision can one be free to act. To draw back from guilt and from choice in an effort to maintain moral purity or godlike invulnerability is to attempt to live secluded in the forest. Life in the town requires an admission that one might be the betrayer of one's friends.

This insight about the self recalls the figure of Judas, whose presence resonates so pervasively in this narrative. In the school play, the disciples of Jesus come to Judas to seek revenge. This scene is reenacted when Gregor is placed on trial by the partisans (there are twelve of these), who accuse Gregor of betraying Leib to the police. In the intensity of their love for their lost leader, they are willing to punish the betrayer by death. Gregor, they imply, has been a Judas.

Why is Wiesel willing for his protagonist to admit the guilt that the murderers of Jews have always im-

puted to them? By implying that Gregor does—or
ought to—embody Judas, Wiesel reverses the Judas
figure. Instead of the devious, malicious betrayer of
his friend, Judas is here the man who suffers the fate
that befalls all persons who dare to act. To act means
to take upon oneself the possibility of failure, of error
and self-delusion, of betrayal, willingly or not, of
one's friends. Gregor admits these possibilities, and
only with such an admission can he be truly free to act
in resistance and rebellion.

In presenting the revised interpretation of Judas,
Wiesel also judges Christianity and its view of Judas.
By making Judas responsible for the death of Jesus
and extending that responsibility to all Jews, Christians have overlooked the ways in which they too are
betrayers. As long as one assumes that only others
can be betrayers, one can commit atrocities.

In telling the story of Leib and of Gregor, Wiesel
remembers and celebrates the acts of rebellion and
resistance that occurred during the Holocaust. By
this means, he imaginatively shapes a world in which
the survivor can live. It is a world that will demand
resistance against any effort to brutalize other persons and any attempt to sanctify death, a world that
will demand rebellion on behalf of friendship, and a
world in which persons are free to be guilty, and
hence are free to act.[3]

IV

In part IV of the novel the scene shifts abruptly to a
winter in New York in the early 1960s. After the war,
Gregor had, by chance, been reunited with Clara, and
with reluctance on her part they were married. When
we meet them in New York, Gregor is ready to aban-
don—betray—Clara and their young child, hoping

thereby to escape the past that enslaves them both. Clara remains obsessed with her love for Leib, while Gregor remains obsessed with memories of Gavriel. Both suffer the deepest pain of winter: loneliness. Gregor has reached an impasse. His efforts to create a new world after the Holocaust have failed, and he is ready to move on and make a new beginning elsewhere. "The only solution," he thinks, is "to go away."

By the close of the novel, Gregor strengthens ties with a religious community in Brooklyn and reaffirms his commitment to his family. He comes to see that "we are alone, yes, but inside this solitude we are brothers." The novel opens with an overwhelming sense of ending but ends with a new beginning as Gregor recovers parts of the world that was destroyed. What Wiesel has done in the entire novel—tell a story that resonates with ideas and incidents from the Jewish heritage—Gregor comes in the final part to do in his own life. For both Wiesel and his protagonist, the key to beginning again lies in retelling and thus reclaiming one's story. One builds a future by bringing the past, transfigured by imaginative remembering, into the present, "a present which constantly expands and exceeds itself."

All the parts of *The Gates of the Forest* move back and forth between the motifs of ending and beginning. Structurally, Wiesel relates the same story four times. Each part begins with the motif of ending. There then follows a new beginning that comes to an ending in each of the first three parts. The final part remains open: it concludes with the promise of a new beginning.[4]

In part IV of the novel the process of beginning again depends on Gregor's encounters with a Hasidic rebbe and a mysterious figure whom Gregor takes to be Gavriel. Both meetings echo an incident in Jewish

tradition, that of Jacob's wrestling with an angel. In
the Biblical story, Jacob, who has been living in a
foreign land because he betrayed his brother, is coming home. The night before he is to cross into his
homeland and reclaim his heritage, Jacob is accosted
by an angel. Their wrestling ends in something of
a draw, but Jacob holds on to his opponent until he
gets a new name, "Israel," meaning "he who strives
with God."

This story is explicitly referred to in one exchange between Gregor and the rebbe. The rebbe
speaks first:

"Jacob wrestled with the angel all night and overcame
him."

"Which one of us is Jacob?" asked Gregor. "And which
the angel?"

"I don't know," said the Rebbe with a friendly wink.
"Do you?"

Gregor is Jacob in that at the end of the novel he
returns home with a new sense of himself. Also like
Jacob, he must come to terms with the meaning of
betrayal. Yet the rebbe is also Jacob in that he must
wrestle with the challenges Gregor and the Holocaust
make to religious faith. And both Gregor and the
rebbe are the angel, for each has a message to deliver:
from the rebbe, Gregor learns that traditional faith
can courageously confront the failure of God; from
Gregor, the rebbe hears and accepts that God Himself
is guilty of abandoning the Jews. Each says something to the other. The rebbe speaks of song and joy,
Gregor of lamentation and defiance; the rebbe speaks
of God's judging man, Gregor of man's judging God.

Both sides of this exchange are important in the
new beginning that Gregor is to make. To some extent, the difference between the rebbe and Gregor is a
difference in their perspectives on time. Gregor

focuses on his own lifetime, and the rebbe's vision extends back beyond the beginning of creation. Gregor does not altogether embrace the rebbe's position, but the possibility for rapprochement with the religious heritage is opened. Gregor comes to see that perhaps the rebbe is more courageous in his faith and affirmation than he, Gregor, is in his despair and negation. The rebbe insists that life must progress beyond Gregor's negativism: "We can't stop there, that would be too easy, too cowardly. . . . In what direction are we to go? Where is salvation, or at least hope, to be found?" Such questions as these are the message that the rebbe conveys to Gregor. Not accepting the rebbe's answers, but claiming the questions as his birthright, Gregor comes in the final paragraph of the novel to pray:

At the appropriate moments Gregor recited the *Kaddish*, the solemn affirmation, filled with grandeur and serenity, by which man returns God his crown and his scepter. He recited it slowly, concentrating on every sentence, every word, every syllable of praise. His voice trembled, timid, like that of the orphan suddenly made aware of the relationship between death and eternity, between eternity and the world.

After this sacred moment the novel arrives quietly at its close, with Gregor at least partially reconciled to his religious heritage.

The novel ends in an intellectual stalemate, for Gregor's questions remain unanswered. But on an emotional level the rebbe and the Hasidic community clearly win. Gregor, like all of Wiesel's protagonists, has been crippled emotionally since the Holocaust. Gregor confesses this when he asks the rebbe, "Make me able to cry." "Crying's no use," the rebbe says: "You must sing." As Gregor listens to the rebbe's stories and watches the Hasidic community break

into joyful song and dance, his feelings and imagination slowly awaken; he gradually feels himself becoming the child that he once was. Dimensions of his old self emerge:

> Gregor ceased to struggle. He looked on, listened, and opened himself. The song went through him and transported him far away, to the place where he, who had been killed by the god of war, was awaiting him. So miracles existed.

The intellectual struggle disappears in the fervor of the community's religious enthusiasm, and childlike openness miraculously returns to Gregor. Despair and negativism succumb to the greater power of story and song (including a bawdy song in Hungarian, the language of Gregor's childhood). Opening himself to richer emotional experience, not his arrival at a satisfactory theological position, enables Gregor to achieve at least partial reconciliation with his religious tradition. From the community he learns that persons can help "one another to go forward without stumbling."

The meeting between Gregor and Gavriel in the final pages of this novel is one of the most puzzling scenes in Wiesel's work. The reader is never sure who this Gavriel is or if he really exists: Gregor may be hallucinating, or he may be mistaking someone else for the Gavriel he had known years before, or he may be talking to himself. The ambiguous encounter between Gregor and a figure he takes to be Gavriel is, however, "enough to force a new beginning."

The rebbe reintroduces Gregor to his religious heritage, and his final meeting with Gavriel leads him to see new possibilities in his personal and family history. Gavriel shocks Gregor into a new awareness that human existence must be lived out in relation to a limited number of persons. As the rebbe reawakens

the voice of eternity within him, the meeting with Gavriel alerts Gregor to possibilities in time. These dimensions join and enrich each other in the self which Gregor is becoming.

This Gavriel compels Gregor to retell again the story of the novel, beginning in Hungary and extending through all the experiences that are recounted in *The Gates of the Forest*. Part IV thus recapitulates the entire story, reminding us that one of Wiesel's major concerns is to affirm the creative and healing power of storytelling itself. When he meets Gavriel, Gregor's position is very much like that of the rabbi in the Hasidic tale that stands as prologue to the novel. All the rabbi can do is "to tell the story," and to hope that the storytelling will be "sufficient."

In retelling the story of his life to Gavriel, Gregor is enabled to claim his life, all dimensions of it, as *his life*. Gregor realizes that his life, although scarred by horror and loss, has been rich and worthy in many respects. Instances of goodness have punctuated his story. Gavriel, Maria, Leib, and others befriended Gregor, and he returned their friendship. As he now reclaims the name "Gavriel," Gregor affirms his own life. Gregor—"he who sees"—can once again be Gavriel—"man of God." His present is united with his past, and he discovers a new unity within the self. And what is the message of this new Gavriel? It is Wiesel's message about the power of storytelling and the healing gift of personal relationships. That story, properly told and properly lived, "must be sufficient."

While the encounters with the rebbe and with Gavriel provide the dramatic focal points for the final part of the novel, two other relationships are more central to Gregor's life. These two unusual encounters awaken him to new possibilities in his more ordinary relationships with Mendel, his friend, and

Clara, his wife. During the conversation with Gavriel, Gregor realizes that, had he to choose between Gavriel and Mendel, he would choose Mendel. To choose Mendel means that Gregor is willing finally to let the dead be dead and to cast his lot with the familiar living figures that surround him.

Similarly, in reviewing the stages of his life, Gregor resolves once again to attempt to build a life with Clara. He sees that the struggle to make a new beginning is unending and that it takes place every day in one's closest relationships. Gregor says to Clara: "The struggle to survive will begin here, in this room, where we are sitting." A new world can be formed in a love relationship:

It is enough that a man and woman give themselves to each other for God to confer his powers upon them and for the world to be brought once more out of chaos.

At the end of the novel, Gregor (now Gavriel) resolves to "take the road home, the road of solid ground."[5] At home, "on the trodden ground," he will resume the struggle against the forces of ending and make a new beginning.

5

••

Choosing Life

Elie Wiesel's works often set forth the options for human existence in the starkest of terms. Life or death, hope or despair, love or hate, involvement or indifference, courage or cowardice, God or man—Wiesel positions his characters before these alternatives and implicitly confronts them with the Biblical injunction, "Choose you this day . . ." (Joshua 24:15).

The starkness of these options is reminiscent of a court of law, and, indeed, judicial metaphors permeate Wiesel's narratives. Issues hang in the balance, with advocates on both sides voicing claims and counterclaims, appealing to evidence for and against. At times it is God who is on trial, as in *Night* and *The Trial of God*. Often it is man, as in *The Town Beyond the Wall*, where Michael's fidelity in friendship is weighed in the balance and the indifferent spectator is brought before the court of Michael's conscience. At all times it is ideas, or, rather, the persons who hold them, who take part in the trial by variously fulfilling the roles of defendant, plaintiff, advocate, judge, and jury. The reader is involved in the situation as well: Wiesel's literature requires the reader to judge for himself. Will it be life or death, hope or despair, responsibility or apathy, community or isolation?

Wiesel does not typically render an unambiguous

decision on these issues. Fascinated by paradox, he often appears to opt for both alternatives rather than deliver an either/or judgment. With his work we are not involved in a rationalistic mode of thought in which logic provides the form for thought and action. Rather, we are immersed in a narrative in which story is the model for the self. A story or a life can contain illogicalities; it does not always obey rational rules. The storyteller is not compelled to choose between options: he can show the existence of both within a character or pursue the reflective process until the force of opposition is either dispelled or contained within the totality of the self.

Wiesel's protagonists repeatedly find themselves in situations that require them to know and choose in life what they cannot know and choose in thought. They must come to terms with questions and commit themselves in action: they know because they "are called upon to act."[1] Hence, while the stance of interrogation is central to Wiesel's artistry, his stories also suggest that one cannot suspend living until one has answered or addressed all of life's deepest questions. However much a person might insist that he "can do without solutions," that "only the questions matter," he must nonetheless commit himself, if not to answers, at least to one path rather than another.

To explore these ideas further, this chapter considers *The Oath*, for this novel clearly displays Wiesel's judicial drama. In the intensity of that drama, we see Elie Wiesel declaring himself as a mature artist who has come to terms with some of the ever-present alternatives with which human beings are faced.

I

Wiesel provides sparse information about setting in

The Oath. We learn only that we are in a city, that it is
autumn, and that the time is the late 1960s or early
1970s. The failure to provide specific information
about time and place implies that for Wiesel all places
and all times are, in a sense, the same place and time:
after the Holocaust. His vocation as a Jewish writer is
to reimagine the possibilities for existence, Jewish
and otherwise, in this post-Holocaust situation.

The Holocaust again hovers above *The Oath*, but
the central characters are not survivors. Wiesel here
deals with the struggles of persons who are "born
after the holocaust," who "have inherited the burden
but not the mystery" of the atrocities. The character
who is so situated is a young man, nameless throughout the book, whose mother survived the concentration camps. He remembers his mother's memories of
the Holocaust. When we meet him in the novel, her
past has robbed him of his present and future, and he
is ready to commit suicide.

The young man yearns to settle his accounts with
life alone, but, for Elie Wiesel, the context in which
the issues of life are finally adjudicated must be that
of the encounter between persons. In *The Oath* the
encounter is between the young man and an old man.
Azriel, now close to eighty years of age, is an engag-
ing mixture of saint and madman. Although he was
not in the death camps, Azriel carries within him the
memory of his own holocaust, for he is the sole survivor of a pogrom that killed everyone, Jews and
Gentiles alike, in the small village of Kolvillàg
somewhere in Eastern Europe early in this century.

The encounter between such human beings as
these is fundamental to Wiesel's vision. Although
they appear to occur merely by chance, these events
carry a dense significance, for "true encounters are
those set in heaven, and we are not consulted." In
those occasions in life when a person senses that all
previous experiences have been but a prelude to the

present moment and all that has come before has
been a preparation for action in this particular situation—in that type of encounter, one confronts one's
destiny. In such a situation, the person becomes
"capable of embracing his whole life and considering
it as one undivided destiny, hanging upon a simple
alternative."[2]

Azriel's response to his encounter with the young
man reflects this aura of denseness and of destiny, for
he feels that this one meeting is the purpose of his existence: "Have I lived and survived only for this encounter and this challenge? Only to defeat death in
this particular case?" He resolves to help the young
man "out of gratitude," as much because of a need to
save himself as because of a need to deliver the other.
He realizes that neither he nor the young man will be
the same after their encounter, for "man changes
whenever he confronts his fellow-man, who, in turn,
undergoes an essential change." Azriel does change:
he emerges from the "closed world of memories" to
act on behalf of his despairing companion. The young
man changes as well: he is diverted from suicide.

The vital context of encounter should be distinguished from two other possibilities that Wiesel considers yet finally rejects. At one extreme, there is the
single individual who, having confronted the external
world and been battered by it, retreats into solitude
to reflect privately on the large issues of existence.
Moshe, another character in *The Oath*, speaks for this
option when he counsels Azriel: "This world is not
beautiful to behold. You will come to prefer the one
you carry inside you." At the other extreme is the
political activist who attempts to solve the fundamental problems of life in the sociopolitical order. Azriel
had followed this path when many years earlier he
looked for salvation in revolutionary ideology. But by
the time the novel's action occurs, he has long since

rejected the political for the personal: "These battles no longer concern me. But your particular choice does. Here I am, responsible for your next step."

The single encounter, so private and limited in scope, carries a significance beyond the two lives that are involved. Indeed, "every encounter suggests infinity." Azriel carries the motif further:

To turn a single human being back toward life is to prevent the destruction of the world, says the Talmud. Do something good and God up there will imitate you; do something evil and suddenly the scale will tip the other way. Let me succeed in diverting death from this boy and we shall win. Such is the nature of man . . . whether he celebrates joy or solitude, he does so on behalf of all men.

Such is the significance that Wiesel places on the meeting of two persons, and in that meeting, as rare and mysterious as it is, the great issues of the human spirit are tested.

This understanding of the importance of the encounter does, however, seem at odds with other currents that move through Wiesel's work: David decides at the end of *A Beggar in Jerusalem* to take up the ordinary life of his friend Katriel by marrying his widow; Gregor chooses at the conclusion of *The Gate of the Forest* to live a "normal life," by which he means that he will work, have a family, be a citizen, and do other pedestrian things. Also, in *The Town Beyond the Wall* Pedro teaches the virtues of "simplicity." With these earlier figures Wiesel seems to suggest that one's character is shaped and revealed in everyday relationships to which we are committed over a period of time. Indeed, on reflection, the notion of a momentous encounter does seem highly dramatic, like something we would expect in the concentrated world of a story but scarcely anticipate in ordinary life. Perhaps we reveal our true character in

those countless deeds that we unthinkingly undertake or fail to undertake on behalf of other persons. The great moments, the decisions made after deep reflection, the momentous relationships—perhaps those are not the proper test of our fundamental life choices.

Wiesel presents both possibilities; but he is not, nor are his readers, compelled to decide in which arena our freedom to act is finally tested and tried. Although *The Oath* emphasizes the momentous, taken as a whole, Wiesel's work suggests that the extraordinary and the ordinary enrich and fulfill each other. To have the one, you must have the other, and the loss of fidelity in either diminishes the human spirit.

Nonetheless, Wiesel's insistence on extraordinary encounters is central to his distinctiveness as a contemporary writer. Some artists remove the truly extraordinary from their work, thus presenting a flattened view of experience and giving their characters no center around which to pattern the moments of their lives. In such stories there is no before and no after, only an interminable middle. There is no variation in the human experience of time. Wiesel's stories modulate between the mundane and the high intensity of such moments as the encounter. In creating moments of true encounter, Wiesel reveals his commitment to the story as the model of the self. Those encounters provide axial points around which life may be organized; they give dramatic shape to one's experience in time; they bring the character to a fresh understanding of who he is and who he might become.

II

The characters' choice in *The Oath*, as in all of Wiesel's literature, is between life and death. When we meet Azriel in the novel he has already chosen life,

while his young companion has chosen death. Azriel insists that "death, on all levels, is not a solution but a question, the most human question of all." He counsels his young companion:

I am not telling you not to despair of man, I only ask you not to offer death one more victim, one more victory. . . . Whether life has a meaning or not, what matters is not to make a gift of it to death.

He has reached this position largely because he has assimilated the thinking of Shmuel, his father, and Moshe, his teacher. In large part, the interior life of Azriel has been a conversation between Shmuel and Moshe. We can better discern the nature of Azriel's choice and its implications for Wiesel's vision by attending to these two formative influences.

Shmuel was the chronicler or historian of the Jewish community in Kolvillàg. When on the fateful night of the pogrom Shmuel entrusted to Azriel the *Pinkas*, the book containing a history of the deliberations and actions of the community over the centuries, he bequeathed to his son the symbol of the principal values of his life: memory, tradition, speech, community. Without these Shmuel could not have existed. They constituted a destiny that he might have denied but could never have escaped.

Moshe presented a vital contrast to the values Shmuel represented. Moshe was attuned to eternity rather than to history. His energies were directed toward transcending this world, not transforming it; he looked to the Messiah who was to come, not to the religious community that already existed. His way was that of the mystic, who by isolation and prayer can serve the community he shuns. Through the power of his own religious intensity, he sought to compel the Messiah to deliver his people from the contradictions and sufferings of history.

Moshe played a pivotal role in the events prior to the pogrom in Kolvillàg. Just before Easter, a ne'er-do-well Christian youth disappeared. (He later reappeared, unharmed.) At first there was little alarm, but soon Christian passions flared, and ancient suspicions rose until action against the Jews seemed inevitable. At that point Moshe stepped forward, hoping to avert the disaster. He first proposed to the Jewish community that he confess to having kidnapped the boy. But when his confession did not satisfy the Christians, he devised another strategy: silence. Moshe persuaded the Jewish community to swear that any persons surviving the pogrom would be silent about it afterwards. Such silence could not remove the threat then hanging over Kolvillàg, but it might have a long-range effect. Telling the story of past atrocities had not prevented new ones, so perhaps silence would stir the conscience of mankind and disturb even the indifference of God in a way that words had not.

In the intensity of his vision, Moshe edged toward madness. Indeed, in Wiesel's work the mystic and the visionary are always somewhat mad, for "true madmen are as worthy as true saints." There are, however, different kinds of madmen, some possessing insights that can be shared, others withdrawing totally into themselves. The danger is that "madmen move inside a system all their own, where they alone can pass judgment." Moshe was slightly mad when he wanted to save the community by means of his death. This was a mad idea because it proposed that a man could take the place of God. A different kind of madness prompted Moshe to propose the plan of silence, for with it he encompassed the entire community within his vision. Through the force of his vision and personality, through the energy generated by his commitment, he moved the community to sacri-

fice its past on behalf of an unknown and uncertain future.

These are the components of the dialectic of Azriel's life. Shmuel bequeathed to him the public record of the religious community, and Moshe initiated him into a secret, hidden tradition. Shmuel directed Azriel to the words God spoke on Mount Sinai, while Moshe wished him to experience the silence which accompanied those words. Shmuel was committed to what words reveal, and Moshe to what is hidden beneath them. Moshe defined the difference between the two men:

I like your father. He and I are trying to attain the same goal. Only our methods differ. He takes care of the past, my domain is the future. He trusts memory, I prefer imagination.

The difference was not that one man stood for life and the other for death. The question was, whose way best serves life? On the night of the catastrophe in Kolvillàg, Shmuel spoke for the last time to his son:

Who is right, Moshe or I? Who sees further? . . . We shall know that when we know the continuation and end of this story.

Before the reader can understand the meaning of Azriel's final choice between these two men, he must understand Moshe's strategy of silence. The meeting between Moshe and Shmuel toward the end of the story about Kolvillàg is crucial to this. After Moshe was arrested, Shmuel, accompanied by his young son Azriel, went to the prison in order to record events accurately for the community. In Moshe's prison cell, the spokesman for history and the spokesman for silence, for memory and imagination, for the past and the future, faced each other. For Moshe, the writing of history had to cease, for

if suffering and the history of suffering were intrinsically linked, then the one could be abolished by attacking the other; by ceasing to refer to the events of the present, we would forestall ordeals in the future.

Silence, for Moshe, was the way to "resolve the problem of Jewish suffering," "without the help of the Messiah."

III

Wiesel's fascination with silence in *The Oath* has several causes. Azriel implies one when he asks, "How was I to speak of what defies language? How was I to express what must remain unspoken?" Language is limited—as Wiesel says in *Souls on Fire*, "all experience cannot be transmitted by the word." Experience forces us to the boundaries of language, and we must finally accept our inability to express the full reality we know. Moreover, Moshe's appeal to silence suggests that speech is always ambiguous. As Azriel remarks, "to speak of it [the pogrom] is to betray it." Language both clarifies and confuses, and it also beguiles. Azriel himself recalls that at one point in his life he forgot the ambiguous nature of language and persuaded himself "that language was omnipotent as the link between man and his creator." As Wiesel bitterly states in *Legends of Our Time*, "language can mend anything"—or at least we can trap ourselves into thinking that it can.

Another factor that surely figured in Moshe's abandonment of speech was his recognition that language in part creates the reality of which it speaks. The poor of the Jewish community knew this and vowed not to speak of the impending disaster, should they survive. Adam the Gravedigger expressed the thought: "In the beginning of evil and

death there was the word. Read the Bible! It's all there! The word announces what it names, it provokes what it described—didn't you know that?'' The simple people and the mad seer agreed that if one does not speak of suffering, it will go away.

These characteristics of language contributed to Moshe's choice against speech. But silence itself may be positive, it may itself serve life. Silence is more than the negative of speech: it has a creative power and domain of its own. Silence may be a more powerful response than speech to some of life's situations. In *The Gates of the Forest* Clara suggests this when she counsels Gregor: "You stop at words. . . . You must learn to see through them, to hear that which is unspoken." Similarly, Moshe maintained, "When the Messiah will come . . . man will be capable of understanding not only the words but also the blank spaces of the Torah. Yes, yes, they are important, those blank spaces." It is, however, self-contradictory to attempt in language to give an argument for silence, and Moshe wisely did not try to convince the community of the superiority of silence over speech. He claimed only that silence was the one weapon against unjust cruelty that the Jews had not tried. Words had failed: the storytellers' stories had only inspired the oppressors to greater injustices. Perhaps silence was the "language" of "a new era."

Another contemporary master of silence, Samuel Beckett, counsels, however, that "it is all very fine to keep silence, but one has also to consider the kind of silence one keeps."[3] Katriel, Wiesel's protagonist in *A Beggar in Jerusalem*, defines two kinds of silence:

I love silence. . . . But beware: not all silences are pure. Or creative. Some are sterile, malignant. . . . There is the silence which preceded creation; and the one which accompanied the revelation on Mount Sinai. The first contains chaos and solitude, the second suggests presence, fervor,

plenitude. I like the second. I like silence to have a history and be transmitted by it.

Is the silence to which Moshe compelled the community the silence of chaos and solitude or that of presence and plentitude? In the confrontation with Shmuel in prison, Moshe initially suggested, that he favors the latter:

The words pronounced at Sinai are known. Perhaps even too well. They have been distorted, exploited. Not the silence, though it was communicated from atop that same mountain. As for me, I like that silence, transmitted only among the initiated like a secret tradition that eludes language.

With these words, Moshe commended the way of the mystic, who walks in the unspoken, unspeakable Divine presence. But he did not stop there:

But even more, I believe in the other tradition, the one whose very existence is a secret. A secret that dies and relives each time it is received, each time it is invoked. Only the Messiah can speak of it without betrayal.

This is not the silence that accompanies speech and that a community shares and passes along through the discipline of meditation and prayer. This is the silence that is discontinuous, that comes fragmentedly to the few ecstatic souls whose disaffection with the world is total. It is the silence of chaos and solitude, the silence not of the mystic but of the madman. Into this silence that is silent even about itself Moshe initiated the community of Kolvillàg. About this silence Azriel must make a decision.

Wiesel brings us to see that silence, like speech, is ambiguous. Azriel admits this when he says, "I should like to remain silent without turning my very silence into a lie or a betrayal." One can betray one's deepest self by silence as well as by speech. As the

pogrom approached in Kolvillàg, Kaiser the mute, a character who had for years practiced the purifying discipline of silence, finally broke his silence to remind the community of this. To the religious leader, he shouted: "It is by keeping silence that you are perjuring yourself, Rebbe!" We begin to realize, as perhaps does Azriel, that "man is responsible not only for what he says, but also for what he does not say."

Moshe perhaps also understood the ambiguous nature of silence, but he chose to use it—to sacrifice the gifts bestowed by language—in a final, desperate effort to save his people from death. He was willing to sacrifice the history of his community in order to save that community. Celebrated as the distinctive legacy of Israel to humanity, history has been the means by which Jews have lamented their adversities and celebrated their survival. In Moshe's view, history—recording and telling stories of the past—serves only to cause further persecutions. Jews, he insisted, turn suffering into a story, and thereby proclaim their "attachment to history" and to suffering. "Now," he said, "the time has come to put an end to it."

IV

Azriel, the sole survivor of the pogrom, has abided by the pledge he made. Having kept silent about the pogrom for fifty years, Azriel must decide whether to keep his oath or to tell the young man about the catastrophe. He must choose the best way to serve life: by keeping silent, or by telling the story.

The decision that Azriel faces about the pogrom is the same one that Wiesel faces about the Holocaust. During his time of decision, Azriel hears two voices: "Memory, insisted my father, everything is in

memory. Silence, Moshe corrected him, everything is in silence." Azriel, like Wiesel, finally tells the story and thus acts against the silence of Moshe. Like Wiesel, Azriel chooses to serve life by telling the story of death. He hopes that the young man will become more responsive to those who live by hearing about those who died. He hopes that the young man will then choose life.

In this decision Azriel fulfills his destiny as one of the people of memory. He sides with Shmuel, who said: "Is oblivion not the worst of curses? A deed transmitted is a victory snatched from death. A witness who refuses to testify is a false witness." Azriel realizes that language, especially storytelling, ties a person to life, that "one does not commit suicide while speaking or listening," that the oath of silence is itself a type of suicide pact for the community. Language, even with all its dangers and ambiguities, is a path to a healing relationship, for it provides not only a framework for human understanding but a bridge to other persons. To choose speech is, for Azriel, to choose life.

Azriel's choice of speech does not, however, imply a complete rejection of silence, for he no doubt realizes that what storytellers have to transmit has to do "with silence as much as with words." Silence is necessary, because there is much that cannot be said; silence reminds people of the mystery of human suffering. But the silence of the storyteller is linked with his words and assumes meaning only in relation with words. For Wiesel, to unite one's words with one's silences is to move toward that perhaps unreachable place where one's speech faithfully makes present that about which one speaks. This is what Azriel and Wiesel wish their testimony to be. As Wiesel writes in *Legends of Our Time*, their attempt reminds the reader to "be careful with words, they're danger-

ous. . . . They beget either demons or angels. It's up to you to give life to one or the other."

V

We have seen the way in which Wiesel's protagonists move toward affirming life. But an affirmation of life must be made with some knowledge, however implicit, of the kind of life that one is affirming. Hints of the kind of life Wiesel chooses emerge in all his writings, but to approach this issue more directly, it will be helpful to examine individually the ethical, aesthetic, and religious aspects of that life. In Wiesel's work these dimensions are related, not opposed to one another. All three are essential, and the loss of any one reduces the wholeness of the human being.

The Holocaust seems to declare an end to what we call the ethical dimension of life. In *The Oath* the pogrom in Kolvillàg serves this function, for it displays the inadequacy of a vision that sees only innocence and perfectibility in human beings. The pogrom in which all ethical precepts were violated demonstrated that all things are possible. The rebbe of the community stated this clearly when he commented, "A Jew must not expect anything from Christians, man must not expect anything from man." To the rebbe and to Wiesel, placing one's faith in man is dangerous, for Jewish history teaches that mankind is too capricious to be trusted. There are persons, however, who persist in an improper elevation of the ethical capacities of man: the "enlightened" Stephen Braun, having dissociated himself from the community in Kolvillàg, embraced a facile humanism and claimed, "I believe only in man. . . . ."

It is foolish to expect everything from man, as

Braun did, and it is shortsighted to expect nothing from man, as the rebbe did. Wiesel's vision of life expects a limited degree of goodness from man because of conscience, that human quality that is basic to the ethical dimension of life. Nurtured in a community, tempered by action and by failure to act, and sustained by the shared memory of one's people, conscience is at once the height of man's dignity and that which makes him aware of debasement. In Wiesel's view, conscience separates the living from the dead, the human from the subhuman. We see this in Azriel's reflection on the death of a friend: "The last glance cast is still that of a living conscience. The eyes of the dead are empty."

For Wiesel, conscience is not an individual affair. The relational or dialogic nature of conscience is suggested when the narrator of *The Oath* remarks, "Whoever says 'I' creates the 'you.' Such is the trap of every conscience." In Wiesel's works, conscience makes possible a meaningful and responsible existence, for conscience is that which awakens a person to the danger of living meaninglessly, nonresponsively, and negatively.

Conscience, for Wiesel, seems to be less an innate faculty than an accomplishment of humanity that each generation learns from the preceding generation. Thus conscience is tied to a specific community and to the past. Memory sustains the individual and collective conscience. The association of memory and conscience is explicit in several places in *The Oath*, such as when Azriel reflects on his memory of the pogrom:

What then is the significance of this mute testimony deposited within me? An invisible force compels me to walk a stretch of road—and we call that life. I look back, and we call that conscience.

Conscience is as much retrospective as it is prospective. The memory of what has been and what might have been allows Avriel to envision possibilities for what might yet be.

The ethical dimension of life is principally concerned with present action in behalf of other persons. For Wiesel, apathy deters persons from such action. Azriel remarks, "I am afraid of only one thing: indifference." This is why he finally tells the story of Kolvillàg: to save the young man from the death-in-life of apathy and boredom and detachment. Habits chain persons to indifference. Azriel's story breaks the habits into which the young man has fallen and restores his attachment to life, enabling him to envision his world anew. As he listens to Azriel, his conscience is awakened and he is released from indifference and opened to other persons.

The awakening of conscience prompts persons to act: it moves Azriel to tell his story. But conscience speaks ambiguously. It counsels Azriel to keep his oath of silence but urges him to speak in behalf of life. Unambiguous direction is impossible, for we are "all too weak, too ignorant to foresee the outcome of our plans." But Azriel realizes that in the struggle of life with death, "one must act, do something." He is called to act. To call and be called are important notions in Wiesel's works: "every word is a call and every call is an adventure," a call to venture one's self in responsible action for another person.

The ethical dimension, which includes memory and conscience, thus is central to the life that Azriel chooses in *The Oath*. With his insistence on these elements, Wiesel stands against the tendency of the past two centuries to free Western society from conscience. Some persons have viewed conscience as a tyrannical force imposed on an existence that should

be spontaneous and unrestrained. Conscience, some have suggested, has contributed to a morbid self-consciousness that should be abandoned. In the Western tradition, conscience has sometimes manifested itself as life-denying rigidity and deadly scrupulousness. Conscience sometimes reduces individuals to a self-enclosed, narcissistic fascination with their own interiority; it can be the barrier to action rather than the impetus. But rebellion against the excesses of conscience in Western culture contributes, as Erich Kahler observes, "not just to a devaluation of specific values, not a mere invalidation of a world of values." Rather, there can be, and Kahler argues that there has been, *"a dwindling of the faculty of valuation altogether . . . a devaluation of valuation as such."*[4]

In retaining conscience as an essential element of the life he chooses, Wiesel reminds us that we cannot and ought not avoid judging our lives. To escape from judgment by means of indifference or moral relativism is to leave open the door to more pogroms and holocausts. If we do not exercise judgment, we refuse the hard task of distinguishing that which serves life from that which serves death. Moshe himself makes this explicit:

To be Jewish is to be able to distinguish. . . . In our tradition, danger is called mixture, the enemy is called chaos. . . . His whole life long the Jew is committed to separating light from darkness, Shabbat from the rest of the week, the pure from the impure, the sacred from the profane, the return from the exile, life from death. . . . *"And thou shalt choose life"* means you shall separate it.

Neither Azriel nor Wiesel would fully endorse Moshe's passion for clear separation, for a fundamental part of Wiesel's vision is that life within history is always a mixture. While we might excuse Moshe's in-

sistence on precision as an indication of his madness, we cannot ignore Wiesel's insistence on the need for judging. To distinguish that which diminishes evil from that which increases it, to discriminate that which contributes to community from that which undermines it, to choose between that which engenders hope and that which erodes it—such judgments of conscience are essential to the life Wiesel chooses.

As Wiesel links the ethical dimension of life to memory and the past, he connects the aesthetic dimension to imagination and the future. The association of the aesthetic with imagination might seem contradictory to his idea of storytelling as an act of testifying. What Wiesel says of *Zalmen, or the Madness of God* applies to all his works: each is "conceived as testimony rather than as a work of the imagination . . . ." As one character remarks in *The Oath*, "All has been said, I can only repeat." In Wiesel's work, the past seems to dominate the future, and certainly "a man without a past is poorer than a man without a future." Memory without imagination is preferable to imagination without memory. Yet in the life that Wiesel affirms a person must have both. Memory and imagination, conscience and dream, past and future work together, each tempering the other, guarding against excess and absolutism. Moreover, the act of testifying is an act of memory *and* of imagination. To bear witness to the past is to imagine and thus re-create the past.

The interdependence of the aesthetic and the ethical is apparent in *The Oath*, for the novel is about bringing to life the young man's imagination as much as it is about resensitizing his conscience. An awakened conscience is the antidote to indifference, and a revitalized imagination is the antidote to despair. Conscience is necessary for action, imagination is necessary for hope, and both are necessary to sustain

a person through a lifetime of action. Azriel says to the young man, "You have not yet lived and already you hate life." He hates life because he fails to see alternatives for the future, for without imagination, people cannot project possibilities in the context of life's necessities. Azriel says, "Make him dream. . . . If I succeed, he is saved. One doesn't kill oneself while dreaming, not even while dreaming to kill oneself." The purpose of Azriel's story and Wiesel's novel is to make us dream, to vivify the imagination and evoke visions of another kind of world, to add "what might be" to "what already is."

For Wiesel, the imagination is inextricably linked to the figure of the Messiah, who connotes a realm so grand that it is called "eternity." As Moshe says, "The Messiah will not die, He is our link to eternity." Wiesel often associates the messianic theme with the image of the child. Moshe says:

We think he [the Messiah] is in heaven; we don't know that he likes to come down disguised as a child. And yet, every man's childhood is messianic in essence. Except that today it has become a game to kill childhood. Thus it is hopeless.

The death of the child, a theme of immense import to Wiesel from *Night* forward, signals the death of the imagination, the future, hope, and the Messiah. *The Oath*, in large part, is concerned with saving the child. Part I of the novel is called "The Old Man and the Child," and Azriel refers to the young man on several occasions as "child." The young man is not literally a child, yet Azriel's story is directed to the element of childhood that is on the verge of extinction in every person. To save the child is to sustain hope; it is to free the imagination to create a future; it is to deny death one more victory; it is to join one's present with possibilities for the future.

But in Wiesel's vision, the imagination and the

aesthetic dimension of existence cannot be allowed sole reign over human life. "To dream," Azriel says, "is to invite a future, if not to justify it. . . ." To justify, evaluate, or judge the creations of one's imagination is the task of conscience. Moshe's error was that he became unwilling to submit his imaginings to conscience for evaluation. He assumed what every madman assumes: that imagination provides its own justification. In *The Oath*, pure imagination is rejected, for unbounded imagination often turns into destructive madness. When the imagination is loosed from the claims of memory and when dream is severed from the restraint of reality, madness may be the consequence.

Wiesel's insistence that imagination be linked with history and memory guards him from total reliance on imaginative powers. We see this in his treatment of Moshe in *The Oath*. As the spokesman for the way of imagination, Moshe's answer to the problem of Jewish suffering was to put an end to history. This is the meaning of his strategy of silence. In a sense, this silence is the medium of pure imagination, for it stands outside the ineradicably historical character of all human speech. In the aesthetic dimension, Wiesel rejects the idea of the pure art work, just as in the ethical he rejects the idea of the pure life. For him, art and life are dramas of good and evil, of time and eternity, of history and imagination.

But important as the ethical and aesthetic dimensions are to the life envisioned in Elie Wiesel's stories, the religious dimension must not be overlooked, for the religious is the center of his life and work. All aspects of life in his work may be found to have religious significance. Life's mystery and ambiguity demand the religious; man is too frail, destructive, and misguided to be the object of his own greatest devotion.

In Wiesel's work, the religious is the realm of the inexplicable and the mysterious. The focus of this dimension of reality is God, and the response to that reality is faith, which may take many forms: rebellion and defiance, gratitude and hope. In Jewish history, God is the source of all life, and to acknowledge God is to acknowledge levels of experience that defy commonsense explanations. God encompasses the depth and mystery of all experience. We see this in a remark of the young man's mother in *The Oath*: "Memory, conscience, the past, fate—God. I am helpless against God." In the syntax of the first of these statements, "God" encompasses the previous four realities, which is not to say that God "equals" the four. Rather, in order to speak adequately of these lesser mysteries, Wiesel must speak of the greater mystery of God.

Wiesel's religious vision, for all its defiance and questioning, is like that of Hasidism, in that it comes to imbue ordinary existence with sacredness. Azriel reports, "It was my Master who had taught me the art of tracking down the presence in our surroundings: all is life, all is symbol." The "presence" is the dimension of God in all things: the *Shekhinah*, the divine presence that according to Hasidism always awaits the attentive spirit. Yet for Wiesel God must be known through human relationships and the events of one's life. The narrator of *The Oath* remarks: "God needs man to manifest Himself, that we know. Whether to affirm His power or His mercy, He does so through man. He uses an intermediary to express Himself and an emissary to punish."

In repudiating Moshe, Azriel chooses to seek God through man rather than to seek Him directly. The rebbe had observed that "consolation can and must come only from God." For Wiesel, God is the ultimate source of all consolation, but that consolation comes

to man through human relationships. Moshe, in his speech to the community, represented the excesses of pure religion when he proclaimed, "Better to speak to God than to man, better to listen to God than to His spokesman." The strategy of silence is an exercise of pure religion, for in Moshe's vision, God understands silence, while man does not. Silence sacrifices the relationship between men to a direct relationship with God, and in so doing it distorts the kind of religious stance that serves life.

Moshe's religious response finally cuts him off from the people of Kolvillàg. While the pogrom raged, Moshe was already imaginatively transported to another place and time: "Moshe in his cell was working on the speech he planned to deliver to the Celestial Tribunal." Moshe had perhaps met with such failure and rejection in his dealings with man that out of despair, not faith, he had set his sight on God at the expense of man. But this is madness, for Azriel's final choice suggests that a man can never be sure that he has done all that he can in the realm of history. Hence one must never desert the human city to secure a place in the divine.

It is appropriate to see Azriel's choice of life as a choice on behalf of God. In his effort to dissuade Moshe from martyring himself for the community, the rebbe made the relationship plain: "You shall live your life, you shall protect it. Whoever renounces his life, rejects life, rejects Him who gives life." Life is to be protected, enhanced, celebrated, and sanctified, because it is given by God: "Life is a gift, and not a piece of merchandise." Life is not at a man's disposal, neither his own life nor that of another. Life must not be bartered away in return for false idols or sacrificed to the wild imaginings of the insane.

Who is God in Wiesel's literature? He is the giver of the mysteries that make up life, and as such He

contains within Himself all the things that He bestows—good and evil, suffering and joy, exile and return, being and becoming, laughter and tears. "What is man? A cry of gratitude. . . . Because of it all, in spite of it all."

These are some features of the life that Azriel chooses in *The Oath*. With this vision Wiesel attempts to enhance our awareness of our shared humanity and to deepen our commitment to time and history. Wiesel assumes the role of a builder who seeks to renew a ruined city. *The Oath* is about the physical destruction and symbolic rebirth of a town, but the larger city for which Wiesel works is the human city. In concerning himself with human existence, Wiesel uses his artistry for the sake of work that will be forever in need of renewal and repair. It is, however, a risk worth taking, for to him any other is a choice of death over life.

6

••

Epilogue

One of the most poignant incidents in Elie Wiesel's stories occurs in *Night* and involves Juliek, a "bespectacled Pole with a cynical smile on his pale face," who is Eliezer's friend in the work camp at Buna. Eliezer and Juliek are among the thousands of prisoners who make the forced march in the snow from Buna to Gleiwitz in January of 1945. The prisoners, exhausted and nearly dead, arrive in Gleiwitz and are crowded into a barracks, bodies stacked upon bodies. In this anguished heap of humanity, Juliek reports his condition to his friend:

I'm getting on all right . . . hardly any air . . . worn out. My feet are swollen. It's good to rest, but my violin . . . I'm afraid . . . that they'll break my violin.

Juliek has carried his violin when other men could not carry their bodies. Later, in the darkness, the prisoners try to sleep. And then

the sound of a violin, in this dark shed, where the dead were heaped on the living. What madman could be playing the violin here, at the brink of his own grave? Or was it really an hallucination?

It must have been Juliek.

He played a fragment from Beethoven's concerto. I had never heard sounds so pure. In such a silence.

113

It was pitch dark. I could hear only the violin, and it was as though Juliek's soul were the bow. He was playing his life. The whole of his life was gliding on the strings—his lost hopes, his charred past, his extinguished future. He played as he would never play again.

In the morning Juliek is dead and his violin is smashed. Juliek's music is a thing both of frightening beauty and of courageous rebellion. Its beauty is heightened because it sounds in the darkest night against the purest silence; its rebellion is intensified because it sounds at the brink of death.

At times, Elie Wiesel's stories resemble Juliek's playing of the violin. Only a madman or a person possessed by hope could think that, in a world of such catastrophe and malignancy, delicate sounds or fragile words might count for anything. Only a person of immense daring would create sonority and form in the midst of disruption and chaos. Wiesel's stories speak against the night of the Holocaust in a sometimes beautiful and always daring way.

Like Juliek's playing, Wiesel's stories disrupt our expectations. We do not expect to hear a violin in a dark shed filled with dying men. Wiesel's story shocks the reader and extends the range of his expectations. In the final pages of *The Gates of the Forest* the rebbe raises the question of expectations to Gregor. He asks, "And what do you expect of yourself?" Gregor replies: "Very little. Almost nothing." Later, Gregor returns the question: "And you, Rebbe? What do you expect of me?" and the rebbe answers, "Everything." By the end of the novel, Gregor comes to expect more from life and hence is empowered to resume "the struggle to survive." The pattern of development of Wiesel's protagonists is contained in this incident: they move toward claiming greater expectations of life.

Wiesel's stories demand a great deal of those per-

sons whom Wiesel calls "true readers" or "true
listeners," those who wish "to enrich their own lives
and to understand them." Wiesel believes that such
readers participate in a story and help "make the
story what it is." The narrator of *The Accident* has in
mind this kind of dialogue between story and reader
when he remarks:

To listen to a story is to play a part in it, to take sides, to say
yes or no, to move one way or the other. From then on there
is a before and an after. And even to forget becomes a
cowardly acceptance.

And again, after relating the story of a child who was
abused by German officers, the narrator comments:

Whoever listens to Sarah and doesn't change, whoever
enters Sarah's world and doesn't invent new gods and new
religions, deserves death and destruction.

Wiesel expects his stories to engage the reader pro-
foundly. The story must surprise the reader and
dissipate the indifference frozen inside him.

The relationship that Wiesel wishes to establish
between the story and the reader is one of interrogation. The narrator of *The Accident* has this in mind
when he comments:

I am a storyteller. My legends can only be told at dusk.
Whoever listens questions his life.

The listener or reader brings to a story habits of
thinking and expectations for life that the story
places in question. The story challenges the reader to
question and allow his ways of understanding himself
and his world to be altered and expanded. "To be a
writer," Wiesel says, "also means to correct injustice." And the only way in which writing can do
this is by effecting change in the thoughts and actions
of the reader. "Once upon a time," Wiesel has said,

it was possible to write *l'art pour l'art*, art for art's sake. People were looking only for beauty. Now we know that beauty without an ethical dimension cannot exist. We have seen what they did with culture in Germany during the war; what they called culture did not have any ethical purpose or motivation. I believe in the ethical thrust, in the ethical function, in the human adventure in science or in culture or in writing.

Wiesel intends with his storytelling to teach, to speak wisdom and voice insight. In all that he writes, Wiesel seeks "to tell of himself while telling of others, to close gaps and create new bonds."

Why does Elie Wiesel write? He writes for Juliek and for millions like him:

One meets a Hasid in all my novels. And a child. And an old man. And a beggar. And a madman. They are all part of my inner landscape. The reason why? Pursued and persecuted by the killers, I offer them shelter. The enemy wanted to create a society purged of their presence, and I have brought some of them back. The world denied them, repudiated them, so let them live at least within the feverish dreams of my characters.

It is for them that I write. . . .

When man, in his grief, falls silent, Goethe says, then God gives him the strength to sing of his sorrows. From that moment on, he may no longer choose not to sing, whether his song is heard or not. What matters is to struggle against silence with words, or through another form of silence. What matters is to gather a smile here and there, a tear here and there, a word here and there, and thus justify the faith placed in you, a long time ago, by so many victims.

Why I write? To wrench those victims from oblivion. To help the dead vanquish death.

Notes

1. NEVER SHALL I FORGET

1. A useful source of information about Wiesel's life and work is *Harry James Cargas in Conversation with Elie Wiesel* (New York: Paulist Press, 1976).
2. The year of the first publication of a book by Wiesel, whether in French or English, is given in parentheses in the text throughout this study.
3. As developed in the middle ages and later, Kabbalism is a complex and esoteric religious system that holds that every aspect of Scripture has a hidden meaning. Of special note for understanding Wiesel's early life is the Kabbalists' concern for a secret knowledge available only to the initiated.
4. Rainer Maria Rilke, *Sonnets to Orpheus,* trans. M. D. Herter Norton (New York: W. W. Norton & Company, 1962), p. 17.

2. THE JOURNEY INTO NIGHT

1. There is also a difference in age between the Eliezer of the story and Elie Wiesel: Eliezer is one year younger than Elie Wiesel was when the events described in the book took place. The discrepancy arose because Wiesel was uncertain when he was taken to Auschwitz whether he was born in 1928 or 1929. Jews in East European countries often did not register birthdates

117

with state officials, hence it was common for a person to be unsure of his age.

2. Lawrence S. Cunningham, "Elie Wiesel's Anti-Exodus," *America,* April 27, 1974, pp. 325–27.

3. THE DRAMA OF INTERROGATION

1. Quoted by Michael Berenbaum, "The Additional Covenant," in *Confronting the Holocaust: The Impact of Elie Wiesel* (Bloomington: Indiana University Press, 1978), p. 236. Berenbaum is citing Irving Rosenbaum, *The Holocaust and Halachah* (New York: KTAV Books, 1976).

2. See, for example, his discussion of Rebbe Levi-Yitzhak of Berditchev in *Souls on Fire,* pp. 89–112.

3. Paul Tillich, "The Lost Dimension in Religion," in *Ways of Being Religious,* ed. Frederick J. Streng et al. (Englewood Cliffs, N.J.: Prentice-Hall, 1973), p. 356.

4. Nathan A. Scott, Jr., *Three American Moralists: Mailer, Bellow, Trilling* (Notre Dame, Ind.: University of Notre Dame Press, 1973), p. 221.

5. Irving Halperin, "From *Night* to *The Gates of the Forest:* The Novels of Elie Wiesel," in *Responses to Elie Wiesel,* ed. Harry James Cargas (New York: Persea Books, 1978), p. 62.

6. Quoted by Frank Kermode, *The Sense of an Ending: Studies in the Theory of Fiction* (New York: Oxford University Press, 1966), pp. 140–41.

7. Quoted by N. Jeffares, *W. B. Yeats: Man and Poet* (New York: Barnes & Noble, 1966), p. 38.

8. Wiesel himself suggests that indifference is not only a sin but a punishment in "Storytelling and the Ancient Dialogue," a lecture delivered at Temple University, November 15, 1969.

9. T. S. Eliot, "Four Quartets: Little Gidding," in *The Complete Poems and Plays* (New York: Harcourt, Brace & Co., 1952), p. 145.

10. Graham Greene, *The Quiet American* (New York: Viking Press, 1956), p. 230.

11. José Ortega y Gasset, "The Self and the Other," trans. Willard Trask, in *The Dehumanization of Art and Other Writings on Art and Culture* (Garden City, N.Y.: Doubleday & Co., 1956), p. 167. This essay parallels Wiesel's views in its discussion of the self, thought, and action. Ortega writes: "Unlike all the other beings in the universe, man is never surely *man;* on the contrary; *being man* signifies precisely being always on the point of not being man, being a living problem, an absolute and hazardous adventure, or, as I am wont to say: being, in essence, drama!" And, again: "Man's destiny, then, is primarily *action*. We do not live to think, but on the contrary, we think in order that we may succeed in surviving" (pp. 173, 174).

4. A New Beginning

1. Wiesel's names for his characters—such as "Gavriel"—are always important, especially those that contain "El-," one of the Biblical names for God. Wiesel has said: "Every main character or rebbe has such a name to show the part of God in the name. If there had been no part of God in man, there would be no problem, no metaphysical problem.... In each character I have a mystical part, therefore he is an 'El-'."

2. "Jewish Values in the Post-Holocaust Future—A Symposium," *Judaism* 16 (Summer 1967), p. 285. Participants: Emil Fackenheim, George Steiner, Richard H. Popkin, Elie Wiesel.

3. In addition to the approach that is presented in this discussion, one could also explore Gregor's confession of guilt in relation to the mystical idea that the Messiah will come to deliver the Jews when there is in the world either one thoroughly just person or one thoroughly unjust person. In part II of the novel, Gregor approximates the just person; in part III, he attempts to be unjust. Wiesel's point is clear: Gregor fails, and the Messiah does not come.

4. It should be noted that the Hasidic tale about storytelling that stands as prologue to the novel has the same structure as the novel as a whole.
5. Gregor's words echo a statement by Martin Buber: "Everything points to the necessity of now attaining once again to a beginning, the beginning of a real life for the real God in the real world." In *The Origin and Meaning of Hasidism,* ed. and trans. Maurice Friedman (New York: Horizon Press, 1960), p. 40.

5. CHOOSING LIFE

1. Johann Gottlieb Fichte, cited by Edward Engleberg, *The Unknown Distance: From Consciousness to Conscience: Goethe to Camus* (Cambridge, Mass.: Harvard University Press, 1972), p. 28.
2. Paul Ricoeur, *The Symbolism of Evil,* trans. Emerson Buchanan (Boston: Beacon Press, 1969), p. 103.
3. Samuel Beckett, *Three Novels by Samuel Beckett: Molloy, Malone Dies, The Unnamable* (New York: Grove Press, 1965), p. 309.
4. Erich Kahler, *The Tower and the Abyss: An Inquiry into Transformation of the Individual* (New York: George Braziller, 1957), p. 203. Emphasis is Kahler's.

Bibliography

1. WORKS BY ELIE WIESEL

Books

The following is a chronological listing of English editions of books by Elie Wiesel. With one exception, which is indicated below, the translation is from the French.

Night. Trans. Stella Rodway; foreword by François Mauriac. New York: Hill and Wang, 1960.

Dawn. Trans. Anne Borchardt. New York: Hill and Wang, 1961.

Dawn. Trans. Frances Frenaye. London: MacGibbon and Kee, 1961; New York: Avon Books, 1970.

The Accident. Trans. Anne Borchardt. New York: Hill and Wang, 1962.

The Town Beyond the Wall. Trans. Stephen Becker. New York: Atheneum, 1964.

The Gates of the Forest. Trans. Frances Frenaye. New York: Holt, Rinehart and Winston, 1966.

The Jews of Silence: A Personal Report on Soviet Jewry. Translated from the Hebrew by Neal Kozodoy. New York: Holt, Rinehart and Winston, 1966.

Legends of Our Time. Trans. Steven Donadio. New York: Holt, Reinhart and Winston, 1968.

A Beggar in Jerusalem. Trans. Lily Edelman and Elie Wiesel. New York: Random House, 1970.

One Generation After. Trans. Lily Edelman and Elie Wiesel. New York: Random House, 1970.

Souls on Fire: Portraits and Legends of Hasidic Masters. Trans. Marion Wiesel. New York: Random House, 1972.

The Oath. Trans. Marion Wiesel. New York: Random House, 1973.

Ani Maamin: A Song Lost and Found Again. Trans. Marion Wiesel. New York: Random House, 1973.

Zalmen, or the Madness of God. Based on a translation by Nathan Edelman, adapted for the stage by Marion Wiesel. New York: Random House, 1974.

Messengers of God: Biblical Portraits and Legends. Trans. Marion Wiesel. New York: Random House, 1976.

Four Hasidic Masters and Their Struggle against Melancholy. Notre Dame, Indiana: University of Notre Dame Press, 1978.

A Jew Today. Trans. Marion Wiesel. New York: Random House, 1978.

The Trial of God: (As It Was Held on February 25, 1649, in Shamgorod). Trans. Marion Wiesel. New York: Random House, 1979.

Some Articles and Addresses by Elie Wiesel

From Holocaust to Rebirth. New York: The Council of Jewish Federations and Welfare Funds, 1970 (12-page pamphlet).

Against Despair. New York: United Jewish Appeal, 1973 (15-page pamphlet).

"Talking and Writing and Keeping Silent," in *The German Church Struggle and the Holocaust,* ed. Franklin H. Littell and Hubert G. Locke. Detroit: Wayne State University Press, 1974.

"On Revolutions in Culture and the Arts," in *Revolutionary Directions in Intellectual and Cultural Production.* New York: Research Foundation of the City University of New York, 1975.

"Art and Culture after the Holocaust," in *Auschwitz: Beginning of a New Era? Reflections on the Holocaust,* ed. Eva Fleischner. New York: KTAV Publishing House, 1977.

"The Holocaust and the Future," in *The Holocaust: Its Meaning for Christians and Jews.* St. Louis: National Conference of Christians and Jews, Inc., 1977.

"The Holocaust as Literary Inspiration," in *Dimensions of the Holocaust.* Evanston: Northwestern University, 1977.

"Freedom of Conscience and the Jewish Holocaust," in *Religious Liberty in the Crossfire of Creeds,* ed. Franklin H. Littell. Philadelphia: Ecumenical Press, 1978.

2. WORKS ABOUT ELIE WIESEL

Abramowitz, Molly. *Elie Wiesel: A Bibliography.* Metuchen, New Jersey: The Scarecrow, Press, 1974.

Berenbaum, Michael G. *The Vision of the Void: Theological Reflections on the Works of Elie Wiesel.* Middletown, Conn.: Wesleyan University Press, 1979.

Brown, Robert McAfee. "The Holocaust as a Problem in Moral Choice," in *Dimensions of the Holocaust.* Evanston: Northwestern University, 1977, pp. 47-83.

Cargas, Harry James. *Harry James Cargas in Conversation with Elie Wiesel.* New York: Paulist Press, 1976

——, ed. *Responses to Elie Wiesel: Critical Essays by Major Jewish and Christian Scholars.* New York: Persea Books, 1978.

Edelman, Lily. "A Conversation with Elie Wiesel." *The National Jewish Monthly* 88 (November 1973): 5-18.

Greenberg, Irving and Alvin Rosenfeld, eds. *Confronting the Holocaust: The Impact of Elie Wiesel.* Bloomington: Indiana University Press, 1978.

Halperin, Irving. *Messengers from the Dead.* Philadelphia: The Westminister Press, 1970, pp. 65-106.

Idinopulos, Thomas A. "The Holocaust in the Stories of Elie Wiesel," *Soundings* 55 (Summer 1972): 200-215.

"Jewish Values in the Post-Holocaust Future—A Symposium." *Judaism* 16 (Summer 1967): 266-99. Participants: Elie Wiesel, Emil Fackenheim, George Steiner, Richard Popkin.

Koppel, Gene, and Kaufmann, Henry. *Elie Wiesel: A Small Measure of Victory*. Tucson: University of Arizona, 1974 (28 pages).

Knopp, Josephine. "Wiesel and the Absurd." *Contemporary Literature* 15 (April 1974): 212-20.

Langer, Lawrence L. *The Holocaust and the Literary Imagination*. New Haven: Yale University Press, 1975, pp. 75-89.

Roth, John. *A Consuming Fire: Encounters with Elie Wiesel and the Holocaust*. Atlanta: John Knox Press, 1979.

Sherwin, Byron L. "Elie Wiesel on Madness," *Central Conference of American Rabbis Journal* 19 (1972), 24-33.

———. "Jewish Messianism and Elie Wiesel," in Byron Sherwin, ed., *Perspectives in Jewish Learning—Volume Five*. Chicago: Spertus College Press, 1973, pp. 48-60.

Index

MODERN LITERATURE MONOGRAPHS

(continued on last page of book)

ELIE WIESEL